SODOM
HAD NO
BIBLE

SODOM HAD NO BIBLE

Leonard
Ravenhill

Offspring PUBLISHERS

www.offspringpublishers.com

Copyright © 1971, 2012
All Rights Reserved

ISBN 978-0-9838105-7-5

Printed in the United State of America

Cover design by André Lefebvre
www.creativeforge.org

Inside design by Lorinda Gray/Ragamuffin Creative
www.ragamuffincreative.com

Available on Amazon.com

OTHER BOOKS
BY THE AUTHOR:

Why Revival Tarries

Meat for Men

Revival Praying

America Is Too Young To Die

Tried and Transfigured

A Treasury of Prayer

Revival God's Way

Some titles may currently be out of print.

Leonard Ravenhill

1907-1994

Leonard Ravenhill was born in 1907 in the city of Leeds, in Yorkshire, England. After his conversion to Christ, he was trained for the ministry at Cliff College. It soon became evident that evangelism was his forte' and he engaged in it with both vigor and power. Eventually he became one of England's foremost outdoor evangelists. His meetings in the war years drew traffic-jamming crowds in Britain, and great numbers of his converts not only followed the Saviour into the Kingdom, but into the Christian ministry and the world's mission fields. In 1939, he married an Irish nurse, and from that union came three sons—Paul, David, and Phillip.

Your young men shall see visions

David Wilkerson,
founder of Teen Challenge,

Loren Cunningham,
founder of Youth With A Mission,

George Verwer,
founder of Operation Mobilization.

These men had "visions" of lost men and obeyed their visions with worldwide results.

To these men I joyfully dedicate this book.

Foreword

LEONARD Ravenhill writes with the power and unction of John Wesley.

It is impossible to read his works and still remain uncommitted. You will love him or hate him because what he says cuts to the marrow of the bone.

Only a few men in our generation are called to be prophets who monitor the church and the priests of God. This Holy Spirit monitoring is the Holy Spirit's way of keeping His house and the priesthood holy and effective.

I think this is Leonard Ravenhill's most powerful book. I read between the lines much of his own anguish, soul searching and consecration. Even when he must be negative, it is done in a positive way with one goal in view-the sanctification of chosen vessels.

Hard hitting books like this seldom make the best seller list, but they carry the stamp and approval of God's Holy Spirit.

If you intend to read this book through, be prepared to end up on your knees.

David Wilkerson
1971

Author's Preface

I OFFER it as my considered judgment that the main reason why we do not have heaven-born, Spirit-operated revival in our day is that WE ARE CONTENT TO LIVE WITHOUT IT.

Lesser "blessings" make us happy. Another bus for Sunday School is all that some ask. A bigger attendance this year at Easter and Christmas elevates the joy of many promotion-geared churches. Others boast in a bigger offering for missions.

But I warn you again that the devil and hell fear none of these paltry flesh-born goals. Revival alone shakes the devil's kingdom, breaks his power, robs him of eternal possessions, and releases his captives. Out of revival alone springs a vanguard of men who will eagerly hazard their lives for His dear sake. Revival alone inspires men to carry oversized loads without a murmur, as did their Lord, men who will blaze new trails where souls by the MILLION NOW SIT IN DARKNESS AND THE SHADOW OF DEATH.

BRETHREN! WHEN WE GET HUMBLE ENOUGH, AND LOW ENOUGH, AND DESPERATE ENOUGH, AND HUNGRY ENOUGH, AND CONCERNED ENOUGH, AND PASSIONATE ENOUGH, AND BROKEN ENOUGH, AND CLEAN ENOUGH, AND PRAYERFUL ENOUGH, THEN GOD WILL SEND US A REVIVAL THAT EQUALS AND SURPASSES THE AWAKENING THIS COUNTRY EXPERIENCED IN THE DAYS OF CHARLES FINNEY.

It is my humble and sincere prayer that these pages will inspire you to search after the lost secrets of the early church. I trust that the character sketches of some of God's greatest revivalists will cause you to seek the anointing of God until you receive it, the enduement from on high without which, even if your theology is immaculate, there can be no heaven-rending outpouring, no earth-shaking revival, no hell-defying power in the church today.

—Leonard Ravenhill

Table of Contents

PART ONE

PART TWO: PORTRAITS OF REVIVAL PREACHERS

Part One

Chapter 1

God Is Looking for Men

DR. CARL F. HENRY, when editing "Christianity Today," posed the following question to some twenty leading Christian thinkers: "Sighting the final third of the Twentieth Century, what do you think it offers the church?" The answer of Dr. Elton Trueblood intrigued me, and here it is: "By the year 2000, Christians will be a conscious minority surrounded by an arrogant militant paganism."

For a while I chewed over that statement and swallowed it, but the result was spiritual and mental indigestion. Meditating on it a bit more, I could see that his assessment also fitted the very day in which we are now living. Further meditation led me to see that there has never been a time since the Calvary-Pentecost birth of the Church that she was not "a conscious minority surrounded by an arrogant militant paganism."

Christianity was thrown to the lions as soon as it was born. It was projected into a world that was under a sophisticated totalitarian system, as Dr. Harold B. Kuhn has noted. Like an infant child trying under its own steam to get out of the Grand Canyon, so the infant church seemed hopelessly walled in by a canyon of world power. To the left was the mighty monolith of the Jewish control of religion. To the right stood the Greeks with their sheer face of intellect and reason frowning on this new thing. Straddling the road ahead sprawled the mighty military octopus of the Roman empire. Would any sane person dare to suggest that the believers of that day were not a conscious minority?

Here is the glory of the Gospel! In a few years' time a handful of socially uninfluential men, with empty pockets and empty hands, turned the world upside down for their Lord Jesus Christ!

What a dramatic difference from the evangelistic approach of this day! The apostles had no gold, but lots of glory. We have lots of gold, but no glory. Thank God for the "mercy-drops that round us are falling," but our man-made efforts have struggled for two generations without producing a Finney-like move of the Spirit, a genuine, culture-shaking revival, where the moral climate of our cities is changed and the impact is felt throughout the entire nation. Our present chromium-plated, over-organized, stream-lined, computerized evangelism is as effective as trying to melt an iceberg with a match-stick.

There is but one way to save this generation. It is the way of the Christ, and the outpouring of the Holy Ghost. If we do not pray to make iron gates yield, we will pray behind iron gates and maybe die before they yield. The Salvation Army shook the world when they marched to the gates of hell singing William Booth's battle song, "We Want Another Pentecost; Send the Fire, Send the Fire!"

I AM NOT SURE WE WANT ANOTHER
PENTECOST, BUT WE URGENTLY NEED ONE

We pause here to get a refreshing and profitable view of the early church as it is portrayed by Dr. J. B. Phillips. As I remember it, he said that the Book of Acts describes the Church of Jesus Christ before it became fat and out of breath by prosperity, and muscle-bound by over-organization. This was the church where people were not forced to sign articles of faith, instead they acted in faith. Here was the place where worshippers did not "say" prayers, they prayed in the Holy Ghost. His final slam is not less biting. These folk did not gather together a group of intellectuals to study psychosomatic medicine, they simply healed the sick!

I am fully persuaded that this electrifying picture of the early church is God's norm for His blood-bought church in every age.

Remember, brethren, that Elijah did not appear until there was an Ahab to rebuke, a corrupt priesthood to overthrow, an Ashtaroth's grove to be pulled down. Daniel was not manifest until Nebuchadnezzar edged near to a massacre of the wise men and then demanded worship of all. John the Baptist's day of showing forth was amidst priestly arrogance, spiritual apostasy, and national captivity to Roman lords. John Wesley emerged as the prophet when English morality and religion had collapsed "to a degree that has never been known in a Christian country," according to Bishop Berkley, in his "Discourse

Addressed to Magistrates," written in 1738, the year of John Wesley's amazing conversion.

History does repeat itself in some forms. Wesley's day and ours have many parallels, and the comparisons are worth noting.

Commenting on alcoholic beverages in Wesley's day, John Fielding called them "this liquid fire by which men drink their hell beforehand." He spoke of the liquor merchants as "the principal officers of the King of Terrors," and declared such men "convey more to the region of death than the sword and the plague." The brewers and spirit vendors of that day were not less lacking in conscience than the purveyors of drink today. What if their profits leave a trail of broken homes and human wretchedness, what do they care? What if they use human blood for mortar and children's bones for bricks to build their mansions? They live too far away from the squalor they cause to hear the dying oaths of damnation that moan from the throats of the expiring liquor addicts.

Most manufacturers are proud of their finished goods. Not so the beer barons. They hide their hoards of human wrecks in jails and a hundred thousand premature graves. Billy Sunday, Billy Nicholson, Sam Jones, and the top-line evangelists of a past generation crusaded relentlessly against this broth of hell that we bottle and guild with a score of lies. No national evangelist today belts the brewers. But wine is still a mocker, and strong drink is still raging. The Great Society still has scads of bowery bums in the major cities. There are still more deaths from liquor every year in the United States than from the fighting in Viet Nam. How can we hold our peace against the drink devil?

The present-day craze for the vulgar demonstration of women wrestlers was matched in the Eighteenth Century by a craze to see women boxing. As late as June 22, 1768, a London paper stated that "on Wednesday last two women fought for a new shift (skirt) valued at half a guinea, in the spa fields near Islington. The battle was won by a woman called 'Bruising Peg,' who beat her antagonist in a terrible manner."

There was also a crippling plague of gambling abroad at the time of the Wesleyan revival. When he turned 21, the famous Oliver Goldsmith was given about $250 to study law in London. It was all swallowed up at a gaming table in Dublin before he ever saw London.

Blood sports were the sport of kings. Nature worship was as well known and practiced then, as natural expression is heralded now. Both are bastards of deism. High society was low in morals. One does not need a law degree to see that these conditions are matched in our day, too.

I repeat, high society was low in morals. George the II, Horace Walpole, and the Prince of Wales were examples of those of the highest class who lived flagrantly and unashamedly in adultery. There is a note from Sir Walpole to his friend, Mann, relating his attendance at a subscription masquerade where George the II was present, and at which a certain Miss Chudleigh appeared "so naked you would have taken her for Andromeda." Such exhibitions were not done in a corner. In February of 1770 the House of Commons adjourned to attend a similar subscription masquerade held in Soho.

At election times bawdy horseplay, obscenity, and shameless immorality in the streets brought swarming crowds of sight-seers to London. Local brewers contributed largely to the carnival. This Mardi Gras atmosphere was copied in the villages as well. In his book, London in the Eighteenth Century, Balleine says that some men "sold their wives by auction in the cattle market, and baptism registers show how rampant was immorality in the villages." The open trade of the prostitutes caused men to classify them as "Drury Lane Vestal," or "Covent Garden Virgin," for example. The ironical name of one such prostitute was "Newgate Saint."

The New York papers said a few days ago that sailors coming to that city are being warned not to walk alone at night, and to avoid certain spots altogether. Was that fear abroad in Wesley's day? Horace Walpole, in a hot letter to Sir Horace Mann, spelled it out this way, "One is forced to travel, even at noon, as if one was going to battle." And Smollett, in his History of England, says, "Thieves and robbers have now become more desperate and savage than they had ever appeared since mankind was civilized."

Over all this camp of devilry there hung the stench of rampart slavery. Wesley vehemently attacked it, as well as those who were making themselves rich at the expense of the poor. Time would fail me to tell of other voices of Wesley's time which are equally matched in our day.

Against this background we see the enormity of Wesley's task. Wesley never expected to be voted "Man of the Year." The flamboyant Beau Nash lampooned him. The celebrated literary critic, Dr. J. L. Hammond, put down Wesley's revival as "a storm in a tea cup." Southey also derided Wesley. This man Southey left a fortune behind him. Wesley left six pounds, six silver spoons, a well-worn minister's gown, a handful of books, and what was the other thing? Oh, yes, THE METHODIST CHURCH!

Wesley lived year in and year out on one hundred dollars per year, this despite unprecedented sales of his tracts. His was the passion of a fire-baptized heart looking through tear-washed eyes and loving with what his brother, Charles, called, "Love divine, all loves excelling."

Preacher, what kind of a gospel have we to present to such a self-condemning people? If our message lacks "THE POWER OF GOD UNTO SALVATION," dare we call it the Gospel?

The English critic, Dennis Potter, says that the church is in a "real and irreversible decline." Another English critic scorns the gimmicks used by some clergymen to get their empty pews filled. He suggests that it might help if cookery recipes were given with the announcements. Still a third critic cries, "There seems to be no end to the idiocies and indignities perpetrated by modern God-mongers in their vain attempts (and note this well—L. R.)

to accommodate the awesome beauty and thrilling terror of the Gospel to the stubbornly secular mind."

Preacher, to no other man on earth does God give such an awesome task as to you. You trade in eternal things. Yours is a calling that angels might envy. To you is given a power that hell fears above all other powers on earth. You are a divine delegate, a God-endued ambassador, a plenipotentiary. Life and death are in your hands. To some your message is a savor of death unto death, but to others your words are a savor of life unto life.

I believe the Christ who cleansed the Temple in the days of His flesh would, without question, cleanse the pulpit if He were here right now.

Preacher! Would He have to cleanse yours?

Chapter 2

Paul's One Thousand Days

PAUL trusted God. God trusted Paul! Trusted him with a vision and with a commission unparalleled in human story.

It happened during the one thousand days that Paul spent in solitary confinement with God (Gal. 1:1-18). This is the best university in the world. The University of Silence. Its secrets are known to God alone. Its place is under His appointment. Its scope and dimensions are hidden from human view until God takes off the wrappers. Its results are immunity from fear, flattery, fame, or fire, and a Holy Ghost inoculation to stand against earth and hell and carnal churches.

Can imagination infer from the Pauline story what inspiration has left out? Is it unreasonable to think that Paul saw an unveiling of the plan of the ages from creation to the consummation? Did he descend into hell and witness the torture of the damned? Did he have a preview of the Judgment Seat of Christ? Was he shown a spine-tingling picture of the Great Supper when the blest will sit down with Moses and Abraham in the majesty of Jesus' presence?

Perhaps "the Lord whom thou persecutest" appeared again to Paul during his one thousand days in the Arabian desert, as He did when Paul was stopped in his tracks on the way to Damascus. But whatever visions Paul may have had, I am sure that among them was a long and unforgettable look at God's unfolding plan of Redemption. Over and against the human heart, which God calls a horrible pit, Paul saw the passion of His Lord, the power of the Gospel, and the possibilities of Pentecost. NO LESSER VISION COULD EVER HAVE CARRIED HIM THROUGH THE PERILS, THE PERSECUTIONS, AND THE SUFFERINGS THAT LAY AHEAD OF HIM.

The scope of Paul's life is breath-taking. Born in the ancient capital of the world, Tarsus, he finished his course in the military capital of the world, Rome. Between the two he spent much time in Jerusalem, the intellectual capital of the world, and from there to Corinth, the sin capital of the world.

Any of us would have considered the successful establishment of a thriving church in a thoroughly corrupted city like Corinth as the crowning achievement of our ministry, but not Paul! No, he desired "to preach in Rome also." What a hurdle!

Rome as Paul saw it was the mistress of the earth, powerful and putrid, regal and rotten, brilliant in civil law but lawless in morality, a city with its gods, its ghettos, and its gutters. Heine is said to have knelt before the statue of Venus de Milo, gazing up at her and saying, "Ah, you are so beautiful, but you have no arms to lift men." So with Rome. Proud, pretty with its terraces, fountains, and arenas, parading its might in the streets, but without power to stem the tide of moral corruption that crippled it and finally toppled it. This city was gripped by philosophies and cults as numerous, and as Godless, as those in Athens, and by depravity and debauchery as prevalent as in Corinth. Paul saw the Roman populace as it really was—a mass of blind souls, practiced in perversity, clever in their conceit, lounging in their lust, defiant in their devilry, violent in their vice, senseless in their sensuality-an empire of souls against whom the wrath of God was soon to be outpoured.

Quite possibly Paul watched the thousands, and tens of thousands, leaving the coliseum, jubilant that once more Christians had provided exciting entertainment for them, and an excellent meal for the lions. Such arenas were the setting for mass murder, where a multitude no man can number were gouged, beaten, eaten, and burned to death for their faith in Jesus Christ. There was no limit to the blood-letting and death-producing tortures which the cultured pagans of Rome so enjoyed. Men were hung on low trees where bears were allowed to tear them to pieces before they expired from the hanging. The believer could mutter a simple formula, "Caesar is Lord," and get out of it, or he could say triumphantly, "Christ is Lord," and enter into martyrdom. Sometimes the pet girl or a prince of the pretty paramour of a nobleman could signal the death of a saint by a mere giggle or a downward flick of her thumbs. Four days of such revelry barely satisfied the angry souls of the damned in their rage against the Christians, and the Roman holidays became more and more frequent. Even the slaves were given time off in order to join the general population, the priests, the vestal virgins, and the senators in an ever-increasing orgy of bloodshed and sadism.

CAN YOU IMAGINE THE APOSTLE PAUL DARING TO STEP INTO THIS CITY OF HATRED AND VIOLENCE WITH ANY LESS COMPREHENSION OF THE POWER OF THE CROSS THAN HE HAD?

He knew every twist of the human heart, every weakness of the human will, and every trick of the enemy to destroy the souls of men. Listen to this page from his diary:

> Moreover, since they considered themselves too high and mighty to acknowledge God, he allowed them to become the slaves of their degenerate minds, and to perform unmentionable deeds. They became filled with wickedness, rottenness, greed and malice; their minds became steeped in envy, murder, quarrelsomeness, deceitfulness and spite. They became whisperers-behind-doors, stabbers-in-the-back, God-haters; they overflowed with insolent pride and boastfulness, and their minds teemed with diabolical invention. They scoffed at duty to parents, they mocked at learning, recognized no obligations of honor, lost all natural affection, and had no use for mercy. More than this, being well aware of God's pronouncement that all who do these things deserve to die, they not only continued their practices, but did not hesitate to

give their thorough approval to others who did the same. (Rom. 1:28-32, Phillips translation.)

Our gimmick-geared gospel would have fallen as flat in that day as it has done in our day. Can you imagine Paul and his party confronting this pagan, wicked hoard with hip-swinging girls and hand-clapping boys singing, "Something Good is Going to Happen to You," or offering them a Prosperity Pack for a donation?

Paul weighed his words very carefully, and with the aid of the Holy Ghost he measured the measureless might of Calvary. His crusade banner, held high, read:

I AM NOT ASHAMED OF THE
GOSPEL OF CHRIST FOR IT IS THE
POWER OF GOD UNTO SALVATION

We preachers today face stark unbelief and opposition to the Christ we proclaim, in different ways than Paul faced at Rome, but ways not less deadly nor less damning. The opposition is well-dressed, and very articulate, and comes from the inner temples of learning.

Preacher, if you live in the splendid isolation of your comfortable swivel chair and paneled office, remember that the folk you minister to, and the young people you are trying to reach, move daily amidst an unbelievable morass of immorality on the one hand, and an intellectual garbage heap on the other. Here's how Ayn Rand sees it:

In philosophy, we are taught that man's mind is impotent, that reality is unknowable, that knowledge is an illusion, and reason a superstition. In psychology, we are told that man is a helpless automaton, determined by forces beyond his control, motivated by innate depravity. In literature, we are shown a line-up of murderers, dipsomaniacs, drug addicts, neurotics and psychotics as representative of man's soul,-and we are invited to identify our own among them-with the belligerent assertion that life is a sewer, a fox-hole or a rat race, with the whining in junction that we must love everything, except virtue, and forgive everything, except greatness.

Reader, what of our day? Has this day slipped up on God unawares? Is He afar off? Can He do exploits? Hear Dean Samuel Miller of the famed Harvard Divinity School:

We simply do not know how to think of God. He no longer acts. We do not find Him responsible for anything. We do not fear Him. He is away. Yet we remain capable of religious fervor and expression. We fill the void with aimless posturings and gesturings which we would direct, if only we knew where the right direction lay. A popular religion hides God with a frantic but superficial piety.

This statement is worthy of more than one reading. Here is despair in a mortar board, gowned and degreed. One wonders what manifestation of God's power would satisfy Mr. Miller and his followers. Should the Lord split Manhattan's famous rock foundation and shatter the

Midas mills of Wall Street? Would a three-year drought bend the knees of this nation?

The thirty-second chapter of Isaiah, verse two, carries a loaded word for this present hour, with our vice programs in full swing, and our church programs featuring voiceless pulpits. Listen to these words: "And A MAN shall be as an hiding place from the wind and a covert from the tempest; as rivers of water in a dry place, as the shadow of a great rock in a weary land." GOD IS LOOKING FOR MEN!

Chapter 3

Sodom Had No Bible

A PHRASE from the pen of the great revivalist, Jonathan Edwards, is biting viciously into my spirit right now. When Edwards describes the justice of God as pointing its arrow at our hearts, he adds that ours is "an angry God without any promise or obligation at all."

That phrase is biting me right now. I cannot push it off nor brush it off nor wash it off. It is biting on the inside.

How right Edwards was! What obligations has God to a people like us whose aggregate sin as a nation in one day is more than the sin of Sodom and her sister city, Gomorrah, in one year?

Again, we must ponder the fact that America has advantages gospel-wise that Sodom never had.

Sodom had no churches.
We have thousands.

Sodom had no Bible.
We have millions.

Sodom had no preachers.
We have ten thousand plus thousands.

Sodom had no Bible schools.
We have at least two hundred and fifty.

Sodom had no prayer meetings.

We have thousands.

Sodom had no gospel broadcasts.

As a nation we are richly blessed with Christian broadcasts.

Sodom had no histories of God's judgment to warn it of danger.

We have volumes of them.

America today is living only by the mercy of God. The only reason we are not smoking in the fire-wrath of a holy God is mercy-m-e-r-c-y, prolonged mercy!

America as a nation (England shares this, too) already has had posted all warning signs, signs that Sodom lacked. The dice is loaded against America.

(1) What Obligation Has a Holy God to a People
who spend one hour in church on Sunday, then walk to the ball park to spend several hours walking in the counsel of the ungodly and sitting with the blaspheming sinners who profane His holy name?

(2) What Obligation Has God to a People
who allow a newspaper stand to have fifty-seven different magazines sporting nude pictures?

(3) What Obligation Has God to a People
who allow Japanese girls to be imported to stand nude as "wallpaper" for some hot city night spot?

**(4) What Obligation Has God to a People
whose government gives millions to support a**
*communist country which, by the very nature of its
philosophy, is pledged to kill the hand that supplies it?*

(5) What Obligation Has God to a People
*who place on their coins, "In God We Trust," then bar
children from singing Christmas carols in day schools
and let a half-dozen people get a local law made to
stop prayers by millions of children in such schools?
(In so doing they let a few local cronies bypass a
constitutional amendment.)*

(6) What Obligation Has God to a Nation
*that is well spotted with poverty but can spend four
million dollars in one afternoon on a Florida race
track? (The statistic is Billy Graham's.)*

(7) What Obligation Has God to a Nation
*who is spending more per annum on dog food than on
propagation of the gospel?*

In my judgment a nation or nations that will go as far
as we have gone deserves only one thing-that is, that the
holy God whom they have scorned accept the challenge
of their prolonged defiance of His laws; that He withdraw
the bountiful crops that they have known; or that since
"whom he loveth he chasteneth," a holy God speedily lay
the rod of correction upon us to save us from complete
disaster.

We have unblushingly forced our way through the Ten Commandments onto the brink of moral bankruptcy. We have feverishly entered into a drunken orgy of spending. Ours seems to be the cry, "How soon can we spend ourselves into financial despair?"

Atom bombs cannot fight off the judgment of a holy God. If God unleashes his fury upon this proud, sin-drunk people, there is not a bomb shelter big enough or strong enough or deep enough or safe enough to keep us from the lash of God's holy anger.

One thing and one thing alone keeps us from complete decay in this hour—the church, the true Church, the blood—washed remnant (that has not bowed its knees to the Baal of materialism and that cannot be intimidated by the threats and scorn of scientific humanism).

After Abraham left off interceding, Sodom perished. While Abraham "stood yet before the Lord," men had a representative before God. While Lot abode in Sodom (backslidden though he was), God still had a feeble representative with men. While those positions were maintained, God did nothing. When Lot went out of Sodom and when Abraham made his final appeal for the ten righteous men and found them not—then the fire of the Lord fell (Gen. 19:24). Sodom perished because it had not a remnant. America still has a tiny remnant.

Brethren, PRAY. Pray as did the Psalmist: "Thou that leadest Joseph like a flock; thou that dwellest between the cherubims, shine forth...and we shall be saved."

That astute politician, President Kennedy, staved off the steel crisis and then staved off the Cuba crises. But Mr. Kennedy and "all the king's horses and all the king's men" will not avert a divine plague. Only repentance by a broken and a contrite church can do that.

If God puts the millstone of our sin around the neck of this generation and casts us into the nethermost depths of hell, that would be but our just desert. Sinners are not aware of this fact, nor would they believe this terror if they were told.

The salt of the earth that is saving America at this hour is the Church. Believers, this is your hour. Believers, arise! Believers, begin now to watch, to weep, to work, to war.

Chapter 4

We Need A Baptism
of Holy Anger

PAUL was angered at the sight of the Main Street in Athens walled in with temples to false gods. In the language of the stately, sleepy Elizabethan English of the Authorized Version, we have Paul's reaction to this sight: His spirit was "stirred within him" (Acts 17:16).

J. B. Phillips gives us perhaps the best interpretation of Paul's reaction when beholding scholarly Athens infested with idolatry. In his translation Dr. Phillips says, "While (Paul) was there, his soul was exasperated beyond endurance at the sight of the city so completely idolatrous."

The Amplified Version says, "Now while Paul was awaiting them at Athens, his spirit was grieved and roused to anger as he saw that the city was full of idols." Ancient Athens, though given to class and culture, was still peddling soul-dope.

Let me make some suggestions why Paul's spirit was roused to anger as he paced the streets and beheld Athens' sin.

Paul was angry at the power of false religion to delude the people.

Paul was angry at the reckless devotion of these devotees to powerless gods.

Paul was angry at the staggering wealth sacrificially given to build temples to frauds.

Paul was angry that Christ was cheated of the love which He should have had from men and women who could have been born of the Spirit of God.

Paul was angry that men with hearts of flesh cried out in vain to gods with hearts of stone.

Paul was angry that the atoning blood of Christ was trampled under foot and scorned as dung.

Paul was angry that the intellectuals mocked at the resurrection and ascension of the living Son of God.

Paul was angry that within a heart's beat of an eternal and inconceivably horrible hell men could eat, drink, and be merry.

Paul was angry that the devil could keep living men captive in chains of fear and lust, and then after this life hold them eternal prisoners in the bottomless pit.

The average believer's complacency towards the lostness of men is appalling. We believers today need a baptism of Paul's holy anger.

There is a tale in Greek mythology of a hydra-headed dragon who emerged from his cave each year, fire-breathing and hungry. A meal-offering of the city's seven fairest virgins or its seven finest young men was the price of this dragon's appeasement. Hungrily this monster ate the offering of virgins or men. When satiated, he retired to his lair for another year.

For false gods (false cults) many people in many countries move out to testify today, not just once a year or once a day, but many times a day. With an appetite far exceeding that of the Greek dragon, this empty-bellied and hell-filling monster of the cults consumes souls. But who cares? It is not a radiant Pentecostal or a zealous holiness brother or an unshackled Baptist who knocks at my door to witness. It is a deluded Jehovah Witness or a messageless Mormon. We have in false cults a horrible picture of lost men seeking lost men to lead them to a lost eternity.

Ask yourself these soul-searching questions:
Why don't we attack?
Why do we fear?
Why do we hesitate?
What chills our urgency?
Have we nothing to communicate?
Are we unsure of our own Biblical knowledge?
Do we lack personal assurance of salvation?
Are we unconvinced that the sinners stand in jeopardy of an eternal hell?

Have we forgotten that even as believers we shall at the Bema Seat be judged not only for what we have done but (and this really hurts) for what we could have done?

In the sins of omission that will be brought against many of us at the Judgment Seat of Christ, there will surely be quite a paragraph of indictments where we have failed to witness. Witnessing is not optional, but obligatory. We Christians are debtors.

More than once I have stood on a platform beside the eldest daughter of William Booth, founder of the Salvation Army. As we sang this composition of her own, I have seen the tears spill down her craggy face.

"There is a love constraining me
To go and seek the lost;
I yield, O Lord, my all to Thee
To save at any cost."

The Marechale witnessed in season and out of season. She proclaimed the gospel in the streets, in the taverns, in police courts, and in prisons where she, like Paul, was cast.

To me it is a shocking commentary on present Christian feebleness that while, in the first century, 120 men could move from an upper-room closet and shake Jerusalem, nowadays 120 churches claiming a like experience of the Holy Spirit can be in one of our cities and yet that city at large hardly know they are there. In our spiritual warfare the churches must be guilty of shooting with dummy bullets. To change the figure, we must spiritually be running with empty freight cars.

It is my deep conviction that the end of the age is upon us. Things are going to develop more rapidly than any of us anticipate. In the light of this, we need to fence off our altars so high that to get to them takes a do-or-die effort.

This is no hour for crocodile tears, for half-baked commitments, or emotion-packed vows. These should never be permitted to clutter our altars.

Most likely if we walked down Main Street today and saw stately edifices dedicated to strange gods (false cults), we would shrug the thing off with the cold-hearted nonchalant comment, "It's a pity that folk have no more sense than to fall for that kind of stuff." Let me repeat: I believe the hour is come when we, God's people, need the baptism of anger.

There is a command, "Be ye angry, and sin not." Too often if the believer does know anger, he knows anger at the wrong time about the wrong thing to the wrong people in the wrong place. His anger is so often self-generated because his pride has been hurt. The faultless image which he carries of his own personal holiness has been smeared. Or he is chagrined at the affront of some who have dared to suggest that his idol of gold has clay feet. We need to remind ourselves again that the holy Son of God, our Savior, was angry with the pigeon sellers and the polluters of His Father's house.

It is not difficult for me to conceive that with millions of heathen perishing, our pot-luck suppers, our shabby gospel films, our bloodless church membership, and our nervous witnessing (plus our self-contentment and self-indulgence) would all come in for a scathing denunciation from the white-heat heart of the righteous Son of God. We might remember, too, that in the Bible story Jesus was angry at the hardness of the hearts of those who meticulously followed the synagogue's law and system (Mark 3:5).

Ours is now the most chronically unhappy world in history. It would be folly to give an aspirin to a cancer patient, assuring him with lying words that this would cure his malady. Equally criminal (in my judgment) is our attempt to appease the soul-hunger of the millions around us by sermons that are not Christ-centered, not born in the burning heart of a yearning preacher, and not wet with the tears of his own travail and anxiety for fallen men.

Our situation is not like walking down Main Street in Athens, where ignorance, superstition, and strange gods held sway to enlighten people. Ours is a far worse and more terrible situation. We have pulled down the old altars to Jehovah and built new chrome-plated altars to Ashtaroth and Baal.

Recently a Minnesota newspaper recounted that at one town in this state the school board has decided to outlaw all association with Christianity in all school programs. There is to be no Bible in their schools, no prayer, no baccalaureate services, no reference to Christmas or Easter or any Christian holiday. Tell me the difference between the situation in this school and what exists in the Soviet Union. (I would be glad to receive the illumination.)

To stir us sickly saints to rescue the perishing, we need the smell of hell. Oh to be like Thee, blessed Redeemer- angry! More than ever we need to cry with Mrs. B.P. Head:

O Breath of Life, come sweeping through us;
  Revive Thy Church with life and power.
O Breath of Life, come cleanse, renew us,
  And fit Thy Church to meet this hour.

O Wind of God, come bend us, break us.
  Till humbly we confess our need;
Then in Thy tenderness remake us.
  Revive, restore, for this we plead.

O Breath of Love, come breathe within us.
  Renewing thought and will and heart;
Come, Love of Christ, afresh to win us,
  Revive Thy Church in every part.

O Heart of Christ, once broken for us,
  'Tis there we find our strength and rest;
Our broken contrite hearts now solace,
  And let Thy waiting church be blest.

Revive, us Lord! Is zeal abating
  While harvest fields are vast and white?
Revive, us Lord, the world is waiting,
  Equip Thy church to spread the light.

Chapter 5

Preacher! Without A "Woe" Do Not Go

PREACHING—"Hell fears it. Earth requires it. Heaven ordains it." So says Hamish Mackenzie in his challenging book *Preaching the Eternities*.

At this dark and serious hour in human history the church is looking on while the world is marching on and the preachers are mumbling on. Since we have decided to run the church our way instead of God's way, our pastors have had to become a jack-of-all-trades. Blessed is the preacher who dares to stand on his own feet.

If God called you to be the janitor, then do the job, brother; but if He called you to preach, take His advice, obey it, and live by it. Acts 6:4 gives you your guidelines: If you are sweating on ten committees, then take all the vitamins you can, you'll surely need them. He called you to preach. He is not obligated to strengthen you for any other task. If the job is "killing" you, check right here: "His yoke is easy. His burden light."

Since we do not elect church officers because they are filled with the Holy Ghost, but rather because they own two Texaco stations and a hot dog stand, then you might run into opposition in claiming your right to seek God face downward and struggle through sweating prayer.

The deacons or elders should visit the sick and even bury the dead. A week is a very short time in which to plunder Eternity for two sermons to be delivered at the week end (not weak end!).

Times many I have been asked to write a book on preaching. I have a standard reply to that request. I do not know enough about it to be dogmatic on so delicate a matter. This is my fiftieth year of preaching since I began doing it as a boy of fourteen in the streets of England. Yet I know so little about it. Hugh Black has a book out so aptly titled, *The Mystery of Preaching*. You might as well tell a man how to run his home as to tell a preacher how to preach.

I have caught a glow from Eternity many times as I listened to the great master preachers of Britain thirty years ago. Compared with these men, all of whom could move and awaken the heart, I am but a prattling child. I missed Hugh Price Hughes, but I remember hearing his son. He was extraordinary. Then, there was Dr. Luke Wiseman. Just to hear him read the Scriptures was something that time could never erase. He gestured as he read them. On occasion he would move graciously from the pulpit to the piano where he would sing his message to an ever-listening audience. Laboring on until in sight of his eighty-eighth year (as did his beloved John Wesley), this master of the art of preaching was never pompous, never proud. He addressed children as well as adults with equal ease. "You know, boys and girls," he would say, "I am like a commander in the last war. I bring myself to attention, make my salute to the Captain of my salvation, and ask, 'What are my orders for today?'"

There you have it—the secret of his freshness in the pulpit: "My orders for today."

Dr. Sangster of Westminster Hall was also a rare breed of preacher. I am told that he practiced every gesticulation of a sermon before the mirror.

If that is true, he still was so fresh in his delivery that one felt he surely lived in the experience described by Charles Wesley's verse, "Spring Thou up within my soul, Rise to all eternity." Times many he showed to this poor writer the vanity of life, and just what to label "the perishing things of clay."

Dr. Martyn Lloyd Jones had a method all his own. His pulpit was not fringed with a choir (usually the war department of the church!). No special music was provided, not even soloists. Yet for many years he held the ears and the hearts of the British folk, and particularly the ears and hearts of the young folk who came in great crowds to hear him.

None of us who sat repeatedly at the feet of Samuel Chadwick can ever forget him. Chadwick was no run-of-the-mill preacher. He was a pulpiteer, a preacher's preacher. The renowned G. Campbell Morgan and he were great friends, but never rivals. Each held the other's remarkable gift too sacred for criticism, or even comparison. And mark you, both were expositors. But Morgan used glowing terms about Chadwick.

Alexander Whyte of St. Georges, Edinburgh, Scotland, has more than once been called "the last of the Puritans."

He was a man of The Book, and of books. No slob at reading, he, like Tozer and many other greats, soaked himself in the mystics. It was said of Whyte, "He was always like a fire on a cold day." Preacher, you might envy that epitaph! His associate at St. Georges was named Black. The quip in their day was. "I went to St. Georges twice on Sunday. Ach! 'Twas the same as ever. In the morning service Black painted us white and at night service Whyte painted us black." I did not hear Whyte. I did hear Black, and to this day could repeat half the message that he gave.

And listening to the late C.S. Lewis, I was fascinated with his message, and stunned by his simplicity. That's preaching!

Preacher, let's all take a day off and examine ourselves, whether we be in the apostolic succession or not. Otherwise Mackenzie may be right when he says, "We have sometimes been guilty of exercising a ministry which could no more produce a new Christian than a skeleton can bear a living child."

He gave some apostles, some prophets, and some pastors and teachers. Abide by your calling, brother. Let not another man's popularity, style, or wide travels disturb you. "To each his own," in ministry. Take Luther's attitude toward his little-known contemporary, Melanchthon, as your pattern:

"I am rough, boisterous, stormy, and altogether warlike, fighting against innumerable monsters and devils. I am born for the removal of stumps and stones (Come back, brother, we need you!!), cutting away thistles and thorns, and clearing the wild forests; but master Phillipus (Melanchthon) comes along softly and gently, sowing and watering with joy, according to the gifts which God has abundantly bestowed upon him."

Of types of preachers and styles of preaching there are many. But the Bible says, "A man's gift will make room for him." (Prov. 18:16) Let no God-called man envy Naboth's vineyard. Preacher, be yourself, with His anointing!

One vow we might make to the Lord, preacher-brethren, is that while we give more time to prayer this new year, we also give more time to reading, especially the Bible, but also some other books as well. Read what provokes, and even what angers at times. Read the ancients and the moderns. If you are anchored deeply enough to the Solid Rock, read a book like. *For the New Intellectual,* by Ayn Rand. She will make you smart, but she represents the new breed. Your teenagers live in her world, even if you do not. Get them grounded.

Want to learn about preaching? Study Ian McPherson's fine book. *The Burden of the Lord.* Take a slice of Alexander Whyte each week in his republished book, *Bible Characters.* His gold never dims. Try P. T. Forsyth for size. He'll show you the dignity and the doom of the preacher. Arthur Pink is fallible, like all men, but he says some wonderful things, too. *The Pulpit Commentary* is worth all it costs, and is, of course, a mine of spiritual wealth for all your days.

Thomas Cook's *New Testament Holiness* should be read through once a year by every preacher, and likewise,

Chadwick's *The Path of Prayer,* and *The Way to Pentecost. Heralds of God,* and *A Faith to Proclaim,* by Stewart, will also make your soul tingle. If you don't want *The People's Bible* for its subject matter, (reprinted by Baker Bookhouse as, *Preaching Through the Bible*), buy it just for the prayers it contains. Parker prayed before each sermon, and they were recorded verbatim. This man had wings!

But shun that abomination, a book of sermon outlines. If God inspired that preacher who wrote the book, why cannot He inspire you? Somebody else's sermon outlines are a pair of crutches, and mostly dead men's brains. Is God obliged to give them a resurrection?

Well, preacher, keep your eye on the Throne, your knees on the ground, and your confidence in the fact that you are "seated with Christ in heavenly places," not fictitiously, but ACTUALLY. Be certain you can also say with Paul, "I coveted no man's silver or gold or apparel" —and I would add to that, "nor his pulpit."

I am convinced that in the current welter of confusion, theological as well as moral, there are still many asking, "Is there any word from the Lord?" They are not interested, preacher-friend, in your theological juggling act, your elastic vocabulary, your re-hashing of some recent political event or the near doom of the stock market. They want the word of Redemption!

The Puritans had a vast concept of the sinfulness of man, but they lacked the victory side of Redemption. Stick to the "Good News." Jesus came to free us, not to frighten us. This is your year, preacher. Live on your knees out of the pulpit, but stand on your feet in it, and boldly proclaim "the acceptable year of the Lord." May God be with you!

Chapter 6

Pentecost At Any Cost

SOME simpleton, trying to fill in the Grand Canyon with a shovel, would evoke gales of laughter and would suffer scorn and unbearable vituperation. No man will ever fill in that hole—not even with any army of bulldozers (never mind a one—man shovel operation).

We Christians are a "holey" people. There are holes everywhere in and about our theology. There is a big hole or gap between what we read in the Book and what we practice. There is also a chasm in our church life. We seem to this hour to be as far removed from apostolic Christianity as the pope is from marriage. We are strangers from the commonwealth of the divine power of Pentecost. We are aliens to that city—moving enduement that was known to our spiritual fathers of the first decade in Pentecost.

I remember on one occasion using a tin of well-advertised paint. The "fast-color, quick-drying, permanent-finish" selling line hooked me. But my experiment was a flop. Was the paint at fault? No, the painter was the transgressor. He did not read the directions, and so the results could not come out right. For an outpouring of the Spirit let us as Christians go back to the Bible directions.

Even before a return to the Bible, we might ask a searing question: "Do we want another Reformation in the Biblical style?" A second, not-too-easy question is this: "Do we really want a Pentecostal visitation of the Spirit that will shatter our status quo spiritually, socially, and economically?" (Let me inject a stop signal here: Unless you can answer yes to both these questions, don't pass on.)

Our investigation into "Pentecost at any cost" is not merely to find an answer to empty pews nor yet to solve that preachers' headache, the Sunday night congregation. It is not merely a short-cut to getting our particular church or denomination on its feet. The answer to that problem is simple—get it on its knees. Our rediscovery of Pentecost may bring these several changes within a church; or on the other hand, it is possible that the new wine might burst the old bottles.

If we want to, we can get back to Pentecost. But the road up this hill of blessing is steep. (I am assuming here that my readers believe the Bible to be the inspired, infallible, imperishable Word of God, and that it is no mere theological cliché to say, "Jesus Christ the same yesterday, and today, and for ever" Heb. 13:8.)

THE PRICE OF REPROACH

Even suggest tarrying and right off some will dub us Pentecostals (as if that matters).

Or, we would get jerking thumbs and out-of-the-side-of-the-mouth comments like this one: "They are trying to be super-spiritual"—an appendage we all would like at the judgment seat of Christ.

Or some might even term us "lazy" for escaping work for some period.

Or if, with our fetters off, we leap for joy—in heart if not on our feet—then out from the critics would come the shattering phrase, "They are drunk." We could hardly take that.

Another reproach might be the fact that the manner of the Holy Spirit and His method of directing worship would be so anti-orthodox that the unmoved believers might be again heard to say, "They are unlearned and ignorant men." The flesh hates to be slighted intellectually by the intellectuals. Can we pay the price of reproach?

Well then, if the reproach is not too great, if the price is not too high, if the sacrifice is not too involved, and if the stigma is not too humiliating, we can consider the next step to spiritual recovery.

THE PRICE OF DISRUPTION

"Of course we do not have to tarry these days," say the expositors, "because," they add, "this is the dispensation of the Holy Spirit." Dispensationally (if one may dare to use that often-abused word) they are right. But I still hold that we need to tarry.

First, take notice that this tarrying would mean a shattering of our own little program. The Holy Spirit is no one's errand boy. The Holy Spirit does not move at our beck and call. He cannot be slighted by frail human will without serious consequence. For spiritual recovery He must be obeyed. Only let calamity come, and we will all want to be spiritual. Stock market addicts miss their shrine of Mammon when there is personal or domestic calamity or a national day of prayer (called usually when there is no other way out). A "rat in a trap" turns many to prayer. But do we pray when we are not in a trap?

We need to remember that wars always bring disruption. In London, England, just after the Second World War, I saw from the outside balcony of St. Paul's Cathedral an ugly slab of concrete far below. The upper crust of that slab was thirty feet thick, the guide told me. Beneath it and in comparative safety, Winston Churchill, his cabinet, and his military advisors, spent many a sleepless night plotting military strategy in an attempt to out-maneuver a crafty foe. Especially was this disruption true when England "was going it alone," and Hitler's flesh-pounding juggernauts were only twenty miles across the English Channel.

While the top brass were thus engaged, the lesser fry were fire-watching. That meant each man had a certain night that, in pouring rain or in hail from falling shrapnel, he would walk the street and, if need be, put out incendiary bombs. It was a risky task. But here was compulsion to duty as well as a bit of the disruption that all war brings.

In the holy war against the devil and his works, can we be choosey in our obedience? Can we pray when we like? Can we seek the fullness of the Spirit when we are so disposed? No! If we are aware that now is the time for God to do a new thing, then precedents will be shattered. This brings us to another hurdle, the third:

THE PRICE OF WAITING

We need this waiting to get it clear in our minds that Holy Ghost visitation would not have to fit into our preconceived theological orbit. We need the waiting:

— for humiliation and for time for a confession of our too-long-a-time satisfaction with our own works.

— to get our spiritual eyes refocused on the holiness of God and the lostness of men.

— to linger until we have a broken and contrite spirit.

— to prove we can master the claims of this materialistic age in which we live.

— to hear again the living voice of the living God.

— to show our utter disregard for our own efforts and our complete dependence upon the living God for deliverance in this sin-dominated age.

— to convince our skeptical friends that we love the will of God, that we long for the favor of God, and that we seek the power of God with more zeal than we can put into our business lives and with greater hunger than we have for food.

— for a sorrowful confession of sin and pleading for cleansing through the blood of Christ. In the divine presence, vows would be made to put wrongs right and to remain submissive to God's revealed will. I believe that then the Spirit would fall.

Is the fire and fervor of the early church as revealed in the Acts of the Apostles the norm for the church of Jesus Christ? We believe it is. Jesus came that we might have life "more abundantly," life with glow and with flow and with overflow.

The Spirit does not discriminate as to a man's position in a church. The Spirit falls on a Saul and makes him a Paul and an apostle. The Spirit endues a Philip, and he turns the city of Samaria upside down and ransacks the devil's kingdom.

Supernatural evidence has accompanied every revival. The external miracles have been greater in some operations than in others. But—and this is the core of the thing—signs and wonders were done; the rationalists and materialists were stirred, and at times silenced. (Heb. 2:2-4.)

To revival there is a peril and pain—pain for the birth of revival, pain from the scorn of others while revival is in progress, and pain when the fire of revival dies down.

Repeatedly the question has been asked, "Why does revival come in a blaze, but to the delight of the critics soon sputter and die out?" The answer to that question could be one or two of these things (at times maybe both): First: Ignorance could quench the Spirit-an inability to hear the voice of the Lord for the next move. Second: Disobedience—this seems the most likely thing to douse the flame that seeks to consume all the dross. There might be other causes such as laziness to follow the close schedule that the Spirit demands, or there might be smug satisfaction that there is now some "life."

Let us remind ourselves again that the early church "moved." In moving, something or somebody must be left behind. The modern Ananias and Sapphira will find the pace too hot and the price too high. To keep the fire of revival burning, we would have to meet together

— daily for prayer and praise. This is what the church in Acts did (Acts 2:42-66).

— daily for breaking of bread. This the early church did.

— daily for prayer. This was their pattern in the early church.

— in the harmony of the Spirit. This was the glow of the first church.

This stringent schedule would be the death of many of our flimsy and unproductive patterns of life. How easily we Christians move along in the light of the lostness of men and their gambling with the certainty of eternal destruction unless they hear and believe. Sloth has seeped into our endeavors. The mesmerism of materialism has almost completely clogged the channel of blessing. We stand condemned.

Almost every Christian without exception knows better than to live at his present standard of spirituality. "My brethren, these things ought not so to be." There is only one way for the church to operate—God's way. The Bible is the blueprint of this way.

Here, then, is the way back to Pentecost and on to glory!

> Quick in a moment, infinite for ever
>> Send an arousal better than I pray;
> Give me a grace upon the faint endeavor,
>> Souls for my hire and Pentecost today!

Chapter 7

Faith Laughs at Impossibilties

Acts 12

PETER in prison! What a jolt!

We are too far removed from the actual scene to catch the atmosphere of dismay the Christians of that day felt. Peter had moved from Pentecost to prison, from jeers to spears. He was guarded by sixteen soldiers. One wonders why such a defenseless man needed such a group to watch him. Could it be that Herod feared the supernatural, seeing he knew that Jesus escaped such a group that guarded Him?

Had Peter been hedged in by sixteen hundred soldiers, the problem would not have been increased nor the escape less sure. Peter was bound not only by two chains, but also by the thick walls of the prison, by the three wards of the prison, and finally by an iron gate.

When Peter is in prison, does the church organize a plan to get him released? No. When Peter is jailed, do the believers offer a plea to Herod or suggest a price to offer the law-makers for his freedom? No. Peter had released others at the hour of prayer; now others must believe for his release.

Right through the book of Acts, which might be called The Acts of Prayer, we find prayer and more prayer. Dig into the book and discover this power that motivated the early church. In the twelfth chapter of Acts we find a group that prayed. Though a host encamped against Peter, in this were these believers confident: there was a God who could and would deliver. The one never-failing rescue operation was prayer.

There was no hedging about in the prayers of those who made intercession for Peter. Prayer was made without ceasing by the church unto God for him. They did not seem to be concerned whether Herod should die or not. They did not pray that they might escape Peter's fate. They were not asking that they have another exodus to a more hospitable country. They prayed for one person: Peter. They prayed for one thing: his release. The answer proves the point: "Whatsoever ye shall ask, ...that will I do."

Some shabby interpreters of this story have said that when the prayers heard that Peter was at the door, they were unbelieving. I cannot accept this assumption. I am sure that they prayed with expectation. I like to think that they were for the moment staggered by the immediacy of the answer. They could be excused if they raised their eyebrows when Peter said, "I got out quite easily with an angel escort." (Next time you pass through the magic self-opening door at your supermarket, remember that the first door to open of its own accord was operated from above!)

Angel deliverances seem to find no place in our modern theology. Perhaps we would like the Lord to answer our prayers with the least embarrassment to us. After all, who expects that the angelic ranks should be disturbed just to bring deliverance to a praying soul? But supernatural results came for many of the praying saints of apostolic days. The Lord geared a property-damaging earthquake to get deliverance for an apostle. Prayer is dynamite.

There is no weapon formed against prayer that can neutralize it. Some things can delay answers to prayer, but nothing can stop the full purpose of God. "Though it tarry, wait for it."

The first requirement in prayer is to believe—

Believe that God is and that "he is a rewarder of them that diligently seek him."

Believe that God is alive and therefore has power—not only for Peter's deliverance, but for ours.

Believe that God is love and that He cares for His own.

Believe that God is power and therefore no power can stand against Him.

Believe that God is truth and therefore cannot lie.

Believe that God is king and that He will never abdicate His throne or fail in His promise.

Reflecting on the story of Peter, I am rebuked, humiliated, chagrined, stung. Why? Because there are some great modern saints, Watchman Nee for one, who for years have suffered and been held captive by communists and others. Many of the saints today are shut up in prison. The same fate has befallen some of God's choice witnesses in Vietnam and in the Congo.

Such perils to other members of the Body demand concern, concentration, and consecration to a committed plan of prayer on their behalf. I fear that prayer has not been made to God without ceasing for these suffering kinsmen.

Mr. Bunyan shows us his Christian held captive by the Giant Despair in Doubting Castle. The key to his deliverance was Promise.

We Christians are in captivity on many levels today—personal, domestic, church, and missionary enterprise. But fetters break and dungeons fall when prayer is made by the church unto God—

- Prayer without ceasing;
- Prayer that might shatter our status quo;
- Prayer that drains us of every other interest; Prayer that excites us by its immense possibilities;
- Prayer that sees God as the One that rules on high, almighty to save;
- Prayer that laughs at impossibilities and cries, "It shall be done;"
- Prayer that sees all things beneath His feet;
- Prayer that is motivated with desire for God's glory.

The praying of the believer can become a ritual. The place of prayer is more than a dumping ground for all our anxieties, frets, and fears. The place of prayer is not a place to drop a shopping list before the throne of a God with endless supplies and limitless power.

I believe the place of prayer is not only a place where I lose my burdens, but also a place where I get a burden. He shares my burden and I share His burden. "My yoke is easy and my burden is light." To know that burden, we must hear the voice of the Spirit. To hear that voice, we must be still and know that He is God.

This calamitous hour in the affairs of men demands a church healthier than the one we have. This blatant manifestation of evil in the youth and in the violation of God's commandments throughout the world calls for a faith that will not shrink.

Can we let our prayer swords rust in the scabbards of doubt? Shall our prayer harps hang tuneless on the willows of unbelief?

If God is a God of matchless power and incredible might,

If the Bible is the unchangeable Word of the living God,

If the virtue of Christ is as fresh today as when He first made the offering of Himself to God after His resurrection,

If He is the one and only mediator today.

If the Holy Spirit can quicken us as He did our spiritual fathers, then all things are possible today.

The seas were boiling, the winds were howling, the sails were tearing, the spars were flying, the stars were hiding, Euroclydon was blasting. The people were cringing and crying, sobbing and sighing. One man alone was praising. All were expecting death, save Paul. Amidst a scene of hopelessness, if ever there was one, Paul cries, "Sirs, I believe God" (Acts 27).

As things seem to fall apart these days, I am going to join Paul. I am going to say in faith, "Sirs, I believe God." Will you join me?

Chapter 8

We Need Another Pentecost

IN THE LAST half-century. Biblical scholarship has given us a whole new crop of New Testament translations and transliterations. In one of these. Dr. J. B. Phillips, in his hard-hitting paraphrase of The Acts of the Apostles, has some meat for men. First, Dr. Phillips thinks the title of the book should be Some Acts of Some Apostles. I think he is right there.

Next, he takes a two-handed grip of a two-edged sword and smites hard with it. He says that this New Testament picture of the first-century church is given before the church became both fat and short of breath through prosperity, or muscle-bound through over-organization.

This church in the Acts, he adds, did not "say prayers, it prayed in the Holy Ghost; it did not write articles of faith (to be signed by its members), it acted in faith; it did not gather groups to study psychosomatic medicine, it healed the sick."

Where, then, and when and why has the church left her charter of supernatural operation? No wonder that Arthur Wallis cries aloud to this generation, "The ways of

Apostolic Christianity must be recovered, or the church of the latter days will never ride the storms that already threaten to engulf her."

In a recent missionary conference in the Orient, I was disturbed to find missionaries who were themselves disturbed over the theology of Karl Barth. I imagined that I could hear the voice of Paul crying, "Who then is Barth? or who is Baultman?" And again, I could hear Paul saying with heat, "Was Barth crucified for you?" Let me make this clear: Karl Barth is not my headache. I confess to having no theological headache at all. I do have a heartache. I do want to ask when the church is going to get even a little concerned at the mighty fever of iniquity that grips all the nations at this time. I want to hear that folk are going to the house of the living God with sackcloth and ashes because of the glory that has departed from the sanctuary.

> The good old Salvation Army still sings,
> Look down and see this waiting host;
> Give us the promised Holy Ghost.
> We want another Pentecost;
> Send the fire!

Well, whether we want another Pentecost or not, we need it. We need God to send another caldron of heavenly lava, spilling out from another upper room to another moribund church group. The world needs to know that there is a God in heaven—even though a pair of smart Russians scoffed at His presence because they flipped around the earth at some 17,500 miles per hour. They had forgotten, I suppose, that they were traveling 36,000 times slower per hour than God's light. "He that dwelleth in the heavens shall laugh."

In my judgment, only a fool would try to equate the Christianity of this present hour with that yearning, burning, scorching, outreaching manifestation of the power of the Spirit such as is revealed in the Acts of the Apostles more than once. These days, the great gulf between heaven and hell seems hardly a more terrifying abyss than that which separates the church and the world. I am of this unshakable opinion that in so-called Christian countries no one is actually reaching the lost in any great proportions.

Let me add this: There is no hope of immediate revival until the lostness of men grips us believers like a fever and moves us to personal and church housecleaning. If ever there was an emergency hour in the history of men, then this is it. If our natural birth rate were as low as the spiritual birth rate, the nation would be panicking. If the nation teetered on the brink of financial ruin as the church wavers on the rim of spiritual negation, statesmen would be sleepless and sweating for a remedy.

The answer to our dilemma is not a new revelation from heaven. The answer is seeking the old paths and digging out the old wells which superior knowledge, human pride, and flat disobedience have stopped up. There is a balm in Gilead. The question is not. Can we afford to pay the price of Pentecost? The question is rather. Can we afford not to pay the price of Pentecost?

Chapter 9

In His Path To Greatness Jesus Suffered An Assignment Of Silence

SOME men are born to greatness, some achieve greatness, and some have greatness thrust upon them," said one of the sages.

These three adornments were all true of Jesus Christ, the Son of God.

First of all, He was born to greatness—born to be the First-Born among many brethren and to be the First-Begotten from the dead. He was born to greatness by Greatness, the Holy Ghost. He was born of the Spirit into the flesh so that we who are born of the flesh might be born into the Spirit.

Jesus Christ also achieved greatness. Even for the Son of God there was growth and suffering and chastisement. Even for our Savior there were obedience tests. He learned obedience by the things He suffered over a span of time.

Lastly, Jesus Christ had greatness thrust upon Him. It pleased the Father to decree that every knee shall one day bow to the Son and that, to the glory of the Father, every tongue in every language shall confess Him. He, the Son, shall be the supreme Judge of the ages.

In a book called *The Hidden Years,* John Oxenham tries to tell us the untold story of Christ's human development. But he fails miserably in the task. The interpretation collapses under the strain of its own fancifulness.

In a classic work, *The Life and Times of Jesus Christ,* Dr. Alfred Edersheim takes almost 1,500 pages to give us his interpretation of the Master's life. By comparison or contrast, the Apostle John takes only twenty-one pages in his Gospel to give the inspiring story of Christ's life. Add these two accounts together and even then, as the Queen of Sheba said, "The half has not been told."

Let us remind ourselves again, for my own good and for yours, that the word mystery is the first word In theological language. Our late beloved Dr. Tozer used to say, "It is always good to have a little mystery on your soul." Agreed! Yet even so, I want to share some thoughts about our lovely Lord Jesus achieving greatness.

Let not imagination run riot here. What God has hidden, let no man try to reveal. Nevertheless, I am concerned in this study to think with you about the hidden years of Jesus' earthly life—that period in which it pleased the Father to conceal the Son.

To me Christ's patient endurance during thirty years of being "forgotten" is fantastic. Who but the blessed Jesus could have stood ankle-deep in wood shavings—silent and inactive amid oppression, extortion, and corrupt religion? Who but Jesus could have kept unbroken silence while eager, strict men, mourning for the delayed arrival of the Son of David, made their loud lamentations at the Wailing Wall?

How often in those years did Jesus visit the Temple and, glancing at His Father's eye, wait patiently for a sign amid vain animal sacrifices that He might declare Himself the Son of God with power?

Assuming that as a young man Jesus had access to the Scriptures, would He not have read carefully of other men's devious ways of approximation to the pinnacles of spirituality?

Jesus, the Son of God who left the Father's glory, would know that Moses took forty years of schooling at a sheep station on the hinder part of the desert. Moses' step downwards from the royal palace would be quite a comedown from chest-dangling military badges. His hand that once rested on a prince's sword now was to rest for forty years on a shepherd's staff.

Jesus' reading in the Scriptures would bring Him to see that His great prototype, Joseph, also did a stretch in prison as his part in the University of Silence to which God takes all his great men. Jesus knew too the removal of Elijah from a hero's part to the three-year rest period of two-meals-a-day wilderness training before stopping Jezebel in her tracks.

"In the volume of the book it is written of me." Do these words reveal that Jesus had read the Book? Or (sublime mystery) could it be true that since Jesus was the Word, all of it was written in His being and that without ever reading it He knew it all? After all, the Father and the Son and the Holy Ghost were co-authors of this infallible Word.

What patience He must have possessed to watch those strutting, insufferable Pharisees. Their daily parade of flesh, their whining prayers at the street corners, their competition to get the most praise from the most people for their holiness (?). As He saw them attempting to steal God's glory, it must have hurt His tender soul. Before calling them "whited sepulchres," Jesus waited long.

I am sure Jesus made caskets for the dead and witnessed many funeral processions, yet He itched for no power to raise the dead. Though He was "the resurrection and the life," yet with infinite patience He awaited the day when He would touch the bier of the widow's son and shake a city with the news of His life-giving power.

Marvelous grace of our loving Lord that unobserved, unknown, and silent, He could stand back in the shadow when a thousand grief's assaulted His soul and called for His voice. On odd occasions men did praise Jesus, saying, "Never man spake like this man." Usually, however, they ignored or opposed Him. But He was anchored and declared, "Lo, I come to do Thy will."

Most of us hate to be under-rated. We may not seek to head the parade, but-and this is our pitiable weakness-we must be in the parade. The paraded piety of the Pharisees got them the praise of men. "They have their reward," commented Jesus.

As true sons of God, we have nothing of our own to defend or promote. Ours is the light task of carrying His burden.

"There are two things to do with the Gospel: believe it and behave it," commended Mother Wesley to her famous sons, Charles and John.

Maybe Jesus mingled in the crowds for months, hearing John the Baptist thundering forth the word of the Lord. If so. His soul would magnify the Lord that the 400 years of prophetic silence between the Testaments had been shattered. Jesus would watch the baptismal scenes with a burning heart as the crowds increased and as the penitents bowed to the Word.

Jesus visited the Temple which He would one day suddenly fill, but He was silent. He made no claims, gave no hints, manifested no power, uttered no prophecy, sought no disciples, asserted no power, destroyed no evils—just waited silent, strong, and satisfied.

But His hour came. One day John declared, "Behold!" and there was a Voice from heaven. His graduation day had come. How His soul must have thrilled to it!

Reader, pastor, are you hidden away and forgotten? No! None is hidden to the Lord's eyes.

Near-exhausted, lonely missionary, are you forgotten and neglected on some tributary of a tributary of the Amazon (or some other river)? Never! It is in His plan. He is fashioning you for eternity. Fellow pilgrim, if the blessed anointed Son of God could wait with patience, and walk with endurance, and wait in the shadows for His Father's vindication, why then should you and I itch for vindication?

Chapter 10

Though Tossed About

IS A CHRISTIAN a football for the devil to kick around? Is he a dead leaf to be caught by an upsurge of wind, and tossed into the air, then the next moment swept downwards into a different course?

In the thermometer outside your window, the mercury races high under the pressure of heat, and in an icy blast it drops below zero. In life's thermometer, is a Christian helpless mercury, controlled by the fluctuations of life, or is he a thermostat with everything in control?

A Christian cannot control his circumstances—they change like the waves of the sea. A Christian cannot always control his emotions-in a moment grieving news may shatter him suddenly. A Christian cannot control his fortunes—they rise and fall with the markets. He cannot control his health-for a time a virus may knock him out. "My heart is fixed," cried the Psalmist David. And because a heart is fixed, the will can be fixed. And because the will can be fixed, a Christian can master his moods.

My point of concern here is the Christian's moods. Does a Christian need to fall into the helpless bondage of his passing mood? It seems many do, but should they? Isn't bondage to moods just what the worldling falls into?

Many a believer's emotions are affected by public opinion and adverse circumstances. But because the tide is running against him for a while, must he succumb to a mood of depression? Is a mood his master, or is he to master his mood? Think you Jesus was moody? Not for one moment do I believe He was.

Come to a lesser mortal, the Apostle Paul. Was Paul ever under the weather, as the moderns say? After his unjust jail sentence, would you ever have seen Paul looking forlorn and wet-eyed?

Paul was continually buffeted! He was buffeted by men—"Of the Jews five times received I forty stripes save one." He was buffeted in his body—"Once was I stoned." He was buffeted by the waves of the sea—"A night and a day was I in the deep." He was buffeted in his nerves- —"In weariness, in painfulness." He was buffeted in his appetite—"In hunger."

Paul was buffeted but buoyant! Stricken but not subdued! Battered but not beaten! Cast out but not cast down! Whipped but not whining! Imprisoned but not impoverished!

Fearful as was his catalogue of suffering, there is in Paul no hint of any attitude of dejection, self-pity, or gloom. He did not just dig his heels in, grit his teeth, clench his fists, and with stiff arms and blanched face decide he had to weather the frightful storm of circumstances.

Paul, I repeat, was buffeted but buoyant) Hear him glory in tribulations, in necessities, in reproaches. The true Christian is radiant amid ruined hopes and sings in the storm.

Samuel Chadwick often had us sing this song at Cliff College:

> Through all the changing scenes of life,
>   In trouble and in joy.
> The praises of my God shall still
>   My heart and tongue employ.
> Of His deliverance I will boast
>   Till all that are distressed
> From my example comfort take,
>   And charm their griefs to rest.
>   (Written about 1690 by Nahum T. Gate.)

On earth the redeemed sing with Cowper:

> Though vine nor fig tree neither
>   Their wonted fruit should bear.
> Though all the field should wither
>   Nor flocks nor herds be there.
> Yet God the same abiding,
>   His praise shall tune my voice.
> For while in Him confiding,
>   I cannot but rejoice.

The worldling is mastered by his moods, and under pressure and oppression his face mirrors his plight and despair. Not so the true abiding Christian. He has a joy

87

unspeakable, a faith unshakable, and a peace that is indestructible.

We sing "A song of deliverance, of courage, of strength; in my heart He implanteth a song." Sing it, brother, for the world has enough woe!

Chapter 11

Why This Suffocating Indifference?

WE CHRISTIANS are debtors to all men at all times in all places. Men are blind—we must lead them. Men are bound—we must free them. Sinful men are spiritually diseased—we must heal them. Godless men are dead—we must raise them from the dead by the Holy Spirit's power.

But we Christians are so willfully smug to the lostness of men! We are chronically lazy and so callously indifferent! As lax, loose, lustful, and lazy Laodiceans, we are challenging God to spew us out of His mouth (Rev. 3:14-19). God pity us, or smite us! Have we a Moses to stand in the gap if God determines to liquidate this sinning age?

Would we stand idly by with smug indifference if we beheld a blind man walking to the edge of a great cliff, when we knew that his slip over the edge would mean certain death? Any person, I am sure, would make a brave effort to pluck that man from disaster.

Why are our feet so leaden in moving to the rescue of those who move relentlessly by to the edge of eternity, and whose one step into it will seal their doom? Why is

VITAL

there at present amongst us this criminal indifference to the lostness of men? And criminal it is!

Have we nothing to communicate? Is our living so inconsistent with our telling? Are we pitiably unsure of the truth of the Bible concerning the lost? Are we so stony-hearted that neither God's promises nor God's threats disturb us? What octopus has us in its grip? Where will our spiritual polio, our slovenly attention to divine truth land us—and others?

"The church is dying on its feet," writes a British unbeliever blatantly. If that is true, and it seems indisputable on its face value, then the reason is that the church is not living on her knees. False cult addicts spread like pernicious parasites as they unwearyingly mill among the millions, parading their evil wares. They hang like barnacles on our doorsteps as they trade dross for gold, error for truth, disease for health, blindness for sight, bondage for liberty, curse for blessing and death for life. Their zeal is wonderful. Their dope is detestable.

We believers rush a score of miles to a religious breakfast or to a gospel banquet, yet in so doing are not aware that a hundred times we have passed the doorsteps of our perishing neighbors. We spend so much time on hairdo's and how-do's that the cultured lost around us are forgotten!

I met a fine party of young Russian Christians in Australia recently. They had escaped from the Soviet Eden via Shanghai and Hong Kong. After their hectic experiences, Australia is paradise.

There is one old lady of the group who is trying to get back to Russia. Is she homesick? No! she is just worship-sick. In her new freedom, she does not find the same spirit of worship that she knew with the Russian Christians in Russia. She prefers the rigors of the old country and the compensation of uninhibited worship there to that of present creature comforts and religious stiffness.

We Christians would be restless to bring souls into the rest which the rest-giving Savior offers them if all of us had the same infatuation for Christ and for soul-adoration of Christ!

Our condemnation is that we know how to live better than we are living. We could be livelier than we are, and should be. We are suspicious of ourselves that our zeal is not according to knowledge. We are short when it comes to love, and long when it comes to excuses.

Some wit has said that our churches are full of empty people. Maybe they are half full of half-empty people. We have life, but not fullness of life; power, but not fullness of power; concern, but not activating concern; fashion, but not passion; interest, but not inspiration; ability, but not availability. We are not expendable to God for our fellow man.

Hear, oh hear, what another said: "If God does not judge the sin of this nation, He will have to apologize to Sodom and Gomorrah." Frightful words, but only because they are true!

The Cuban situation has kept America on her toes but not on her knees. We tremble for our skins but not for our sins. We feared the mighty midget—Khrushchev-but not the Almighty God.

D. L. Moody said, "I would rather awake a sleeping church than a sleeping world." Our indulgences condemn us! We have slept too long, eaten too much, spent more than we have needed to—on things that did not matter, at prices we could not afford.

The Bible parable says that while men slept, the enemy sowed tares among the wheat. A boy who rises at 4:30 in the morning to deliver papers is considered a go-getter and will get a place in the sun. But to urge our young people to rise at 5:30 to pray is considered fanaticism.

A woman who is doing the rounds—golf, bridge parties, dancing—can give seven or eight hours a day to these testy trivialities. But a woman giving the same hours to prayer and tract distribution is talked about as religiously off-balance.

The man who clips 30 dollars a week out of his budget for cigarettes, drinks, and gambling is considered a sport and worldly-wise man. But the brother who, in love for his Lord and for lost men, tithes the same amount, not only hears whispers that he is being milked by the lazy preachers, but is looked upon as a fool by his workmates. No wonder somebody has written:

"I dreamed that somehow I had come
To dwell in Topsy-Turvydom,
Where vice is virtue, virtue vice;
Where nice is nasty, nasty nice;
Where right is wrong, and wrong is right;

Where white is black, and black is white."

Our whole sense of values must be revolutionized. Before we stand for judgment at the bar of God, we need to sit in judgment on ourselves (I Cor. 11:31). We need to redirect our talents before they are everlastingly taken from us. This is the hour! Tomorrow may not be ours.

Men in Berlin are feverishly digging tunnels to escape the curse of Russia. All men are racing to beat atom bombs. Yet they stagger on blindly without one chance here or hereafter to escape the fiery wrath of God, who is unchangeable in His holiness and in His anger!

I ask again, Why then this suffocating indifference to the lostness of our cultured heathen who sleep away their few sabbaths in their garden seats, or laze by their swimming pools with a peace that is merely moral palsy?

The Bishop of Montana says, "The Church must realize that unless every congregation sets out to do something about its own conditions first, and then about its own community, foreign missions are ridiculous even though they are commanded."

Wind of God, come and blow upon this suffocating indifference that chokes the channel of service to lost men!

Chapter 12

Pentecost

LORD Montgomery, that unpredictable British Field Marshall, said recently that England went into the Second World War equipped to fight the First World War. This was a polite way of saying that in World War II England was way behind the times in battle equipment and strategy.

When Sir Christopher Wren designed the great St. Paul's cathedral in London, he planned a thing of lasting beauty and unfading charm, but did not order it air-conditioned. When George Stephenson built his Rocket engine, it was not a smooth, herculean diesel, but a low-powered hissing machine. In other words, both Wren and Stephenson underestimated the needs of our day, and designed for their day.

Many today have a benevolent patronage of the Church of Jesus Christ (or what they mistakenly think is the church of Jesus Christ). These "wise ones" think that the psalm-singing saints are as much out of line with the atomic age as a penny-farthing bicycle would be on a motor-crowded four-lane highway. Was Jesus Christ guilty, then, of underestimating the need of this twentieth century? Is the Church which Christ founded a cumbersome, slow-moving thing, badly needing a gigantic overhauling and a government subsidy to get her up to date and moving? No! The church does not need state support.

We concede, however, that the Church does need a mighty overhauling by divine Hands, that is, she needs the baptism with the Holy Ghost and fire. When the Lord Christ ascended into heaven from Mt. Olivet, He charged His disciples that they should "wait for the promise of the Father"—the "baptism of the Holy Ghost" with its resultant power.

This promise was exclusive—"Ye shall receive power." Who was to receive the promise? Only the followers of Christ.

The promise was exciting—"Ye shall receive power." In eager anticipation of this blessed enduement, the waiting ones would see all their weakness evaporating in the baptism of fire.

The promise was explicit—"Not many days hence."

The promise was expanding-This thing was not to be done in a corner, nor whispered among the redeemed. It would reach out through them to Judea, Samaria, and the uttermost parts of the earth.

This promise was exalting—In the whole world of created things there is no greater power than that of the Holy Spirit of God. They were to be filled with the Spirit of the living God. Earth has no greater honor than that.

Angels, behold and wonder!

Everything in the heavens above, or in the earth beneath, or in the waters about the earth—all these are

the work of His fingers and this Mighty or
condescends to come and indwell mortals.

But though Pentecost meant power to th
also meant prison to them. Pentecost meant enduement
it almost meant banishment. Pentecost meant favor with
God—it also brought hatred from men. Pentecost brought
great miracles-it also brought mighty obstacles. Pentecost
brought anointing for the upper room preachers—it also
brought appointing for a deacon and under the enduement
he turned Samaria upside down.

In Europe Pentecost Sunday is always called
Whitsunday (White Sunday), and the children usually
dress in white. The disciples were "made white" at the
first Pentecost—that is, their hearts were "purified by
faith" (Acts 15:8,9). This purification is a lost accent these
days in interpreting the Baptism with the Spirit. Under
the title of Spirit-filled churches, there are some weird
and wanton things operating at present.

If too much stress has not been made of the gifts of
the Spirit, then too little has been said of the fruit of the
Spirit. Note how few books are available on the fruits of
the Spirit, but how many on the gifts of the Spirit. Yet the
Son of God said, "By their fruits ye shall know them."

The first essential for the coming of the Holy Ghost
into a heart today is that the heart should be cleansed
from sin, for the Holy Spirit does not fill an unclean heart.
What God has cleansed. He then fills. Finally, whom God
fills, He uses. A holy life is the authentic sign of being
filled with the Spirit.

Today we need a revival of holy living. Why do we have to hang a sign outside our church to announce that we are Fundamental and Biblical? Because without a sign, no one could identify us? When I passed through a town that a few days before had been torn apart by a tornado, I assure you I had not to be told a mighty wind had cleaved the place. A fire is self-announcing. A conflagration needs no publicity. When the fire of the Holy Ghost falls again and the mighty wind of the Spirit comes (I am positive He is coming), then our "bush" will burn, too, and a Moses will turn again to see the great sight. Even so, come Holy Ghost! Come quickly!

Chapter 13

No, No!
It's Not An Easy Road

AS SOME of my readers know, this title, "No, No, It's Not An Easy Road!" is taken from a popular Christian song. Some of my friends dislike it, and rightly so if it is a bit of self-pity sung to the tune of a whimper. This title does seem to bring with it a let-me-cry-on-your-shoulder atmosphere. It badly needs spicing with a touch of militant joy—Paul's glory—in-tribulation type. In the daily-living context of many Christians today, there is no need to blush over this title.

But purge the title of all its sentiment, drain it of all self- pity, cleanse it from its overdose of emotion, and you are left with the bald fact that if one follows the footprints of our New Testament forebears, the true Christian life is anything but an easy road. But "He giveth more grace."

At this moment, I seem to have one eye on this typewriter and the other eye on Hong Kong, where I stayed just a few days ago. There one sees daily the shattered lives of refugees, standing in long lines for soup, and fresh from the brain-washing surgery of Communist conquistadors.

In China the legions of "lost" Christians could repeat tales of suffering equal to anything martyrs of the past have known. I am sure, too, that those living in the paradise(?) of Soviet Germany could also tell us some harrowing tales. Again these things remind us that the Christian song "No, No, It's Not An Easy Road" is not always flimsy, nor always rooted in self-pity.

The life of every Biblical Christian is one of battle. It can be fought joyfully, knowing victory is assured; it can be lived triumphantly, knowing He goeth before. It can be lived recklessly. C. T. Studd and a host of others have demonstrated this.

One false presentation of the sanctified life is that it makes all life an easy victory, a "walk-over." The most sanctified life that this stricken earth has known was the life of Jesus Christ. Was it a walk-over?

To say that the Christian life is an easy road smells either of compromise or ignorance of the Christian way, or both. The purveyor of the "easy road" philosophy does not know his Bible; neither does he cause Satan much trouble.

If you still think that the Christian way is an easy road, then try these seven tests of Christian character:

TEST ONE:

"If thine enemy hunger, feed him." The natural thing is to say that my enemy is hungry because he is not following the Lord as I am, or else to say that his hunger is a judgment from the Lord. In other words, the natural thing is to think that it is my enemy who is the one being tested. But the Lord says my enemy is hungry in order that I may be tested to see if I will obey His divine injunction.

TEST TWO:

"When thou makest a dinner or a supper,...call not... thy rich neighbors." When you and I have a party, do we leave out (with clear intention of doing so) the people that we dislike or the ones from whom we will get no return invitation? Do we really call in the poor? Or do we just sit around with the in-laws and "our little group" and feel somewhat better than the others? If we do, we are leaving this fringe group wondering where practical Christianity comes in.

TEST THREE:

This test is Spiritual enough. I refer to going the second mile. Of course you cannot go the second mile unless you go the first. Within my own heart I am sure the reason that so many of us lack joy is that we lack the keeping of just such a commandment—for such it is!

Are you a second-miler? Would you risk your neck to lift a bleeding man from a robber-infested road, walk with him a second mile, and then for sheer joy that you were doing the will of the Lord, go a third mile and pay his expenses at the inn?

TEST FOUR:

This test can pinch a little, too. Do I esteem others better than myself? There is an awful peril in the Christian life in wanting to pass ourselves off as being better than we are. What is our real estimation of ourselves? Do you and I esteem ourselves better than we are?

I beg you to notice that this Scripture does not state, "say people are better than yourself." Maybe they are not better than you are. But the word is: Honor them, esteem them as though they were dignitaries far ahead of you.

Christ is our Head. Whoever of us hurts another Christian hurts Christ first. Any pain done to a lesser member brings pain to Christ. Shame on us that He should be wounded in the house of His friends!

While sitting in a throbbing jet the other day, eight miles above the earth's surface, I thought of the sparkling truth of Charles Wesley: "Thou, O Christ, art all I want." Wesley had gone far in not seeking esteem for himself.

TEST FIVE:

"As ye would that men should do to you, do ye also to them." How easy is this admonition for us? Do I really change places in my thinking with every soul and with his problems and circumstances? Am I really walking the Pauline way that "thinketh no evil" in my judgment of him? Are all my actions and reactions to the other man with mercy and with judgment?

TEST SIX:

This is a stiff test of my Christian character: Do I handle the other person as though he were Jesus Christ in disguise? Remember the words of the Master: "I was an hungered, and ye gave me meat: I was thirsty, and ye gave me drink: I was a stranger and ye took me in: naked, and ye clothed me: I was sick, and ye visited me: I was in prison, and ye came unto me."

This is shaking information. Our passing up the Christian in his need the other day was our slighting of Christ. Does that make us wince? If in one of our churches Jesus Christ turned up in person, ill-clad, sickly-looking, and in sore need of refreshment, there would be no real need to ask anyone to take Him home to dinner, would there? Some of God's children may be less attractive, but they are His. That is the point. To neglect His children is to neglect Him.

TEST SEVEN:

Do we take up the Cross daily and follow Christ? What it costs us personally to do the will of the Lord is not always what hurts. On the contrary, it is what it will cost others for us to do His will.

There will come times when we will have to leave good and inviting company because at that exact time the Lord demands that we get away with Him. I am sure that if, when He calls, we will not turn aside from company, neither will the Holy Spirit come to us preachers just at the time we want Him.

A strong, eager fellow will quit the ball game at the sight of a girl who fascinates him. How the girl enjoys the fact that she has this pull over the young man. And is it not that way with the Lord, for He says that the secret is with them who fear and obey Him. God does not shout His secrets over a public address system. To hear God, we must be still and alone. Spiritual progress and spiritual maturity depend upon individual obedience, individual vigilance, and individual love of His will.

Do I have the fullness that it takes to follow the Scriptural path here outlined? Somewhere amidst these challenges expediency is going to raise its voice. After only one uplifting exercise in this holy way, reason is going to insert an alternative. The voices of those others who are not willing to tread where the saints have trod and are not wanting us to shame them in their lethargy will most likely begin to whisper to us something rather nebulous called "over-spirituality."

We must despise diversions. Death to self-interest, self-pity, self-seeking, and all the other hyphenated human frailties must be followed by the fullness of the Spirit. The Holy Spirit must fill and flood and flow through the heart. Only then is it possible to fulfill our high calling of God in Christ Jesus.

Nor is this a once-and-for-all fill up. The tense of the verb in Ephesians 5:18 is present continuous and is best translated "Be being filled with the Spirit." The Holy Spirit inflowing and overflowing and outflowing—here lies the secret of victory. Praise the Lord, this fullness takes care of all tests!

No, no, it's not an easy road. These seven tests have proved that it is not an easy road. But it is a great road. "Brothers, we are treading where the saints have trod"— the road that leads to glory. Hallelujah!

Chapter 14

The Significance of Emptiness

IN HIS BOOK Lost and Found,[1] Russell L. Mast speaks in simple and stirring language of the central need of our generation. I quote from his preface concerning what is sometimes called "the beat generation."

Members of this particular generation have turned their backs on the eternal rat race, the "phony" world of make-believe, the "bourgeois civilization." They have made an entirely valid protest against the house of tinsel playthings which a civilization of fabulous wealth has built. Unfortunately they have become rebels without a cause, bearded eccentrics with dirty sweaters, holed up in run-down tenements and cold-water flats. Having failed to find meaning anywhere, they are content to leave the world as it is, seeking only to deaden the pain of having to live in it. In other words, they are prepared to assert the ultimate nothingness and meaninglessness of life.

I urge you to read that quotation again. It has the smell of the morgue about it. It cries aloud with the significance of emptiness. It screams "Bankrupt!" to our generation. As Mast suggests in his book's moving sub-title, "The Search

---

1 Russell L. Mast, *Lost and Found*, Mennonite Publishing House, Scottdale, Pennsylvania.

for Significance," there is today a basic fundamental need to find significance in life.

The worshiper attending an average church these days might leave the place either chilled, thrilled, or filled. If he is a stranger in the city, merely drifting into a steeple house of which he has no previous knowledge, he runs the risk of meeting stern ritualism, dry formalism, leaky liberalism, or stark sensationalism. The house of worship he attends might be filled with incense or with nonsense. The sleepy intonation of the preacher may make the visitor think he is in a funeral service. Perchance the breathless gesticulating orator behind the desk makes him wonder, if he has found the "abominable showman." All these Sunday morning rituals add up to the tragically misnamed thing called worship.

Wherever ritualism prevails, the worshipper, tired from the brainwashing of radio and TV, will turn unfilled to the street again. Were sensationalism reigns, the nerves are further edged and the spirit left vacuous. Where the rich Word of the living God is ministered in the anointing of the divine Spirit, the hungry sheep look up and are satisfyingly fed.

Modern man differs from the returning prodigal. In the first place, our smooth-tongued neighbors do not know that they are lost. Second, if they do awaken to that distressing discovery, they have no idea where the Father's house is or, as Faber puts it, that "the heart of the Eternal is most wonderfully kind." When the prodigal in the far country "came to himself," he at least had his home address and knew that the father was there. He persuaded himself that "the old man" would not turn him out again to drift. This is often not so in our day.

There are voices today that drown out the wail of modern man's lostness and emptiness-the blare of motor horns, the squealing and strident voices on TV, the frantic yells from the sports arenas (often augmented by the voices of Christians who could not raise a cry for a lost world if they tried). Yet for all those who have ears to hear, the lostness of modern man is being shouted from the housetops. Nothing is more evident today than the lostness of people who have no faith in God. Man has severed his connections and his moorings in God.

But is there no genuine thrill in the house of worship, or, for that matter, in the private sanctum of the follower of the Lamb? I think there is. I sensed it today. My heart beat a little faster, my soul soared, my heart leaped, my bowels of compassion were moved. By what, you may ask? By the astounding fact that my heart's cry is heard in the ears of Him who heard the cry of Jonah from the "belly of hell," as Jonah called his blubber bed. In this hour of a sick church and a dying humanity, I am stirred again to think that the Mighty One, who looked in compassion and bent low in power to the minority man on Carmel, hears the cry of us revival-starved souls.

As pre-teenagers, we used to sing with rollicking abandon:

"We've a story to tell to the nations.
That shall turn their hearts to the right."

"Is your story true?" asks a critical world as it gazes on the stultified church of this day. "Is it transforming? Is it the answer to our modern dilemma?" From the throats of burning martyrs comes back the answer: "We gave our lives because Christ's blood is able to save and transform to the uttermost."

Karl Marx once wrote: "Philosophers have only interpreted the world differently; the point is, however, to change it." And none but Jesus Christ can change the world. None but those who have experienced salvation can carry a contagious message of life. It is the saved who are to herald the good news to the lost.

Thronging our streets or hiding from reality are, as Russell Mast says, "bearded eccentrics, lost and lonely," plus millions of unsaved church members. To reach these souls is not the work of hired preachers who have a flair for the sensational. To reach them is the work of every born-again soul who knows the forgiveness of sins and the mighty moral and spiritual transformation by the Holy Ghost.

Dr. Tozer's barbed words, written years ago, have been my traveling companions around the world: "Since the fall of man, the earth has been a disaster area; and everyone lives with a critical emergency." Yet many believers live as if this world were a playground instead of a battleground.

My mailbag has a letter today from a missionary who says that men are being redeemed by Christ's blood and renewed by the Holy Spirit. Until recently, these people were believed to be beyond moral transformation and incapable of grasping spiritual truths. What the gospel can do and is doing for the wild heathen abroad, it can do for the weak pagans at home.

"Tell it around, let it abound.
There's life in the risen Lord."

Chapter 15

Time To Awake

THE PALE, pathetic, powerless, patronized Protestantism of this hour is as far removed from our apostolic faith as is a snail from a seraphim.

All men, from politicians to preachers, sense that there is something dreadful coming upon the earth. I was in Australia when I read the text of President Kennedy's State of the Union address. He said that he was "staggered upon learning this harsh enormity of the trials through which we must pass in the next four years."

The Bible says: "Not forsaking the assembling of ourselves together, as the manner of some is; but exhorting one another; and so much the more, as ye see the day approaching" (Hebrews 10:25). If we are to exhort one another more, then we shall have to meet together more often. Despite this, church meetings grow fewer. There is not to my knowledge a shred of Biblical evidence for this go-to-church-one-day-a-week-for-one-hour practice.

It seems that the glory of Israel was the presence of the Lord. Work and every other thing took a second place. It seems too that the glory of the church in the Acts was also the presence of a miracle-working God plus the daily expansion of the church.

I remind myself again that Sodom had no Bibles. Sodom had no preachers. Sodom had no churches. Sodom had no intercessors (except Abraham, who, I am sure, never set his feet amidst its wickedness). Sodom had no church histories such as we have to warn of God's wrath or to show His interventions in national affairs after prayer and humiliation. Despite all the things that Sodom did not have, yet she perished. Jesus said, "As it was in the days of Lot...even thus shall it be."

We moderns have out Sodomed Sodom in our iniquities. We have turned a blind eye to the piety of our founding Fathers. We have turned a deaf ear to the stirring pages of church history and to their ominous warnings.

We have millions of Bibles in the land and hundreds of stately Bible schools. We have small country churches and stately city church edifices. Our air is jammed with Christian broadcasts. Yet despite these precious possessions, we rate higher than ever in iniquity. Our blatant sinning cannot go on forever without divine judgment.

There is a cowardly Christianity which, despite its lack of zeal for the lost or concern for the mass of heathen, still comforts its fainting heart with a hope that there will be a rapture—perhaps today—to catch us away from coming tribulation. God did not have any such rapture for the Chinese Christians in 1940, nor for His dear children in Hungary, nor for His blood washed who were again blood washed in the uprisings in Russia. But we darlings—fat, faint, and flourishing-think to get to heaven without a scar or even a scratch, if you please.

Perhaps our lethargy has crept upon us and our fraternal security drugged us because we looked for a visible enemy to attack us. And since the Commies have not yet started slugging us as we enter church, we have assumed this is divine favor and have pulled the watchmen from our towers.

Let's face the virus of carnal continuity which perils the church.

Our spiritual fathers went to the martyr fires for things we "footsy" with. There was something vigorous and victorious about their faith. Some of these martyrs were impoverished by the loss of their civil rights; many of them were imperiled by their obedience to Christ. A numberless multitude were imprisoned. They took it all in stride and followed the Lamb withersoever He led them.

As I flick over a few pages of church history, I see the stirring spiritual fight of the Scottish Covenanters. I see the shining faith of the French Huguenots and the stirring fortitude of the suffering Armenian Christians crushed under the iron heel of the Sultan of Turkey. Then I ask myself, "What pressures of persecution could my generation of Christians stand?"

A man who started to paint his front porch while His house was on fire would be considered an idiot. Is the picture overdrawn when I say that this is what the modern church is doing?

Recently a national day of prayer rescued the great and, I think, near-revival country of Brazil from the clutches of Communism. The Commies expected an easy take-over. They had the new currency and headings of their new government paper printed. They reckoned on everything except one: the church of the living God. This they discounted and scorned. For days prayer was made for the country, and a national day of prayer instituted that God would intervene and save the nation from Communism. He did just that.

We need a national day of prayer to save the evangelical church from worldliness and sleepiness. It is time to awake out of sleep! Isn't it pathetic that folk have to be lured to church by the bait of a dessert luncheon to pray for the heathen? Then, too, what of the endless parties, bowling alley trips, etc., that eat our time and erode our souls? Will this type of Christianity stand the hammer blows that will soon fall upon us?

Severe as the storm will be, I know that many will stand. Already they have their loins girt. If I could peep into jails in China within the next hour, if I could snuggle beside my Christian brother on his mud floor in a Siberian concentration camp and hear him humming a hymn of praise; if I could slip into Poland and share some clandestine prayer meeting-my heart would rejoice.

I am sure that the storm is coming, but the angry seas and the roaring waves only show up the greatest skill of the seaman.

Brother, gird your loins, trim your lamp, and go out into the darkness.

Chapter 16

Our Chart and Compass

WITHOUT a qualified guide, no mountain climber would attempt such an ambitious enterprise as the conquest of Mt. Everest. Before he reaches the upper areas of the Himalayas, which are shrouded in mists and blizzards, and have concealed crevices, he must cross a wilderness of ice. Every mountain climber knows there is but a step betwixt him and death. He may have the best climbing gear, his chart and compass may be the last word in efficiency, but still he needs a guide.

Modern ships are equipped with radar; some are loaded with sounding gear. Yet they are compelled to carry chart and compass, and at certain points must take a licensed pilot aboard.

Dare we as Christians attempt to walk the lonely heights of spirituality in the coming year without the chart of the Word of God and the guide of the Holy Spirit? Is the sea of life that is before us less dangerous than the choppy ocean before the Atlantic liner?

It would be a good thing if, at the beginning of what must be a very fateful year in the affairs of men, we would say with the patient Job: "I have esteemed the words of his mouth more than my necessary food" (Job 23:12).

Once again in many parts of the earth, the Word of the Lord is being blamed, burned, or banned. History is repeating itself. But God's Word is imperishable and infallible. Even in this super-scientific age we have no apologies to make for the Bible. It is God's final word to man. It is at the present God's only word to man. It is an infallible revelation from an infallible God to fallible man.

Any society which obeys the Bible's ten basic commandments can stand. Any society which disobeys these divine decrees will fall-however buttressed with wealth or military might.

A few years ago, amid the pomp and circumstances of the coronation of the present Queen Elizabeth of England, there was a pause in the ceremony. Then her Majesty was presented with a copy of the Bible and these words: This is the greatest treasure that earth affords. How true!

The blessed Word of the living God is more than a book of texts. It is also a textbook. The Bible is the only textbook which has charted the whole pathway for every man who has his back to the City of Destruction and his face to the City of God.

The Christian's pilgrimage is uphill all the way, and the staff upon which he leans is the Word of the Lord. The child of God must bear the burden and heat of the day, and the well of comfort from which he drinks continually is the Word of God. The Christian's way is dark, and the Word alone can be a lamp unto his feet and a light unto his path.

All life has its hazards. Wild beasts of the forest devour each other; cats pounce on mice; dogs kill cats; men kill dogs. Even the silent trees have their enemies. To all "life" there is the ever present danger of a greater power.

The socialist says his enemy is undisturbed wealth. The school teacher seeks to destroy ignorance. Medical science battles with disease. Some wage war with untiring zeal against class distinctions and race-color barriers. The Christian life has more hazards than them all.

The Christian knows that to antagonize him and assail his march to heaven, there are at least three great powers; the world, the flesh, and the devil. To combat these mighty foes, a merciful God has given us yet three greater powers: the blood of Christ, the Holy Spirit, and the Word of God. Just now I am thinking particularly of only the third power, The Word of God.

A Christian's muscles and sinews will strain under the loads which the Spirit will give. To insure spiritual stamina, each believing burden-bearer must eat the strong meat of the Word.

Satan, the enemy of souls, snipes pilgrims from behind some innocent-looking bush. A return volley must be given with the same weapon that the conquering Christ used—"It is written." We overcome the devil by the blood of the Lamb and the word of our testimony. The sword of the Spirit must be ours, too.

There is an inner reading of the Word of the Lord. In order to have this, the Holy Spirit, the Author of the

Word, comes to indwell the believer and interpret the Word. Jesus said that man cannot live by bread alone.

But mankind, does not even try to live by bread alone. He drinks at forbidden springs, steals forbidden fruit, and tries to slake his soul-thirst with forbidden stimulants.

Yet he who has embraced God-made prohibitions is glad that the Spirit Himself, the Teacher, the Eternal Wisdom, condescends to take of the things of Jesus and reveal them to us.

The only problem in Christianity is living it. The best Christian is not necessarily a theologian with a mind as keen as a razor. To live the life that God honors, we must first read the Word, then we must obey it. This means that we must practice the Word, that knowledge must be transferred into action. "Be ye doers of the word and not hearers only," said our great Teacher.

Therefore, let us read the Bible to be wise, let us practice the Bible to be holy, and let us obey the Bible to be blessed!

Chapter 17

Wanted:
Men to Ignite the Church

PENTECOST turned volatile Peter into a victorious preacher, for "when the day of Pentecost was fully come..., Peter, standing up with the eleven, lifted up his voice and said..."

Peter not only said; he did. Scarcely had Peter's Pentecost thunderings died away before Jerusalem was filled with his name, along with John's, because both Peter and John channeled power from the resurrected Christ to the "man lame from his mother's womb, whom they laid daily at the gate of the temple called Beautiful." Peter stretched forth his hand, and the life of God within him galvanized the impotent man. (Later just the shadow of this great Peter healed the sick.)

But any man with power in any field also needs power, I am sure, not to use that power. Only a Holy Ghost-controlled man could be trusted with the mighty Holy Ghost power. Too many of us would use that power to our own ends.

The first serious opposition that the elated disciples received was from the schoolmen of the Church, not from the market men. The healed man, leaping and praising

God, startled the temple worshippers. His praises that shattered the vault-like silence of the temple, also shattered the arguments of the ecclesiastical commission who had been sent to investigate this miracle.

The world scorned; how the theologians sneered, saying, "These men who have worked this miracle are unlearned and ignorant." Glorious ignorance! Peter, mark you, wrote two fine epistles. The other apostle, John, wrote a Gospel and three epistles; then for good measure he added a book which still baffles the wise men—The Revelation of Jesus Christ.

But it was not all joy. As Adam and Eve fell in the ideal atmosphere of Eden and as Judas fell while in the ideal companionship of Jesus, so Ananias and Sapphira "fell" while living in the blaze of the descended Spirit.

Until then the Church had been without spot or wrinkle or any such thing. But now it was like old Rome. Once the Roman orator, Cato, tense and terrible, pointed with his index finger over the Mediterranean Sea to North Africa and screamed: "Carthage must be destroyed!" But Carthage was not Rome's real enemy. Carthage did not destroy Rome. Rome was corrupted from within, not from without.

So with the early church. Attack on her from outside was easy to detect. But it now needed the Spirit's discerning through Peter to detect a subtle effort to destroy her from within.

Perhaps Ananias had been filled with the Holy Ghost weeks before his sudden death. But this land sale was no accidental cupidity. Peter knew that Ananias had a Satan-filled heart. This couple did not lie only to the apostles. They tried to fool Deity. They lied unto the Holy Ghost (Acts 5:3). They tried again in lying to God (Acts 5:4). They tempted the Spirit of the Lord.

It is noticeable that it was God who pronounced Ananias' death sentence, not Peter. God slew Ananias! Then Peter, seeing what God did to Ananias and knowing that his wife had schemed the deception with him, had no hesitancy in passing the same doom on the evil woman.

Peter ministered to the impotent man at the gate Beautiful such as he had, in the same way he ministered to Ananias and Sapphira. His ministry was a cure to the impotent man and a curse to the fraudulent couple. To the one it meant life; to the other, death.

Either the spirit of God or the spirit of the devil, it would seem, dominates every living soul. As Jesus said, "He that is not with me is against me" (Luke 11:23).

If this unhappy couple could live near the cauldron heat of the apostolic outpouring and play the hypocrite, then in our day it must be a thousand times easier to do the same thing. If judgment began so early in the church of the living God (when only two of the believers were false), one wonders why judgment is withheld today.

After the chaff was swept from the Pentecostal church by the gale of the Spirit, we read, "Great fear came upon all the church" (Acts 5:11). How could it be otherwise? Who could forget going to morning worship and seeing a man and his wife in the fellowship carried out dead? What a memory for any children present! No wonder great fear came upon them. They were filled with awe. How truly amazing to go to church where the manifest power of the risen Savior was such that some actually died and were dropped in the potter's field, and some came to life in the Spirit. Exciting, to say the least. The whole outcome of this incident was a revival (Acts 5:14).

When Sapphira arrived three hours after her husband had expired, the early believers were still worshipping. What sustained them? Surely there can be but one answer—Christ in the midst. He who had promised to walk in the midst of the seven golden candlesticks and to be in their midst stood before them. There He was— living and loving, enlightening and inspiring. To drag out a meeting for three hours will not bring the Holy Ghost. But when the Holy Ghost is master of ceremonies, who would want to leave?

Alas, We have so crudely tried to "customize" the blessed Holy Spirit. In the New Testament, is there a clue to show that we are right in our one-hour-in-the-morning or our one-hour-a-night Sunday worship? Someone has said that modern preachers have been able to do what the church has not been able to do for 2,000 years-make Christ appear dull.

On the day of Pentecost the world did not stone the men who were "full of new wine." It just scorned them- "Drunk!" Yet it takes such "drunk" men to ignore the world and ignite the Church. God, send us an army of them!

Chapter 18

The Devil

The Whole World Lieth In The Evil One

IN ORDER to cloud the thinking of men about himself, that painfully putrid person, the devil, has poisoned pens and monitored minds.

"All the objections raised by philosophy against the devil are not against him as portrayed in the Bible but against false conceptions of him invented in the past," says Professor Ebrard rightly. These false conceptions did not all get their birth with the medieval artists. Those brush addicts splashed on our minds, as well as on their canvas, a grotesque and utterly unscriptural picture of his satanic majesty.

Dr. VonHuene, Professor of Paleontology at Tubingen, helps us here. He says, "The comical figure with horns and cloven foot attributed to the devil during the Middle Ages and frequently even today in speech, art, and literature is at the least playing with fire; it is sheer flippancy. The danger is far more serious, and his power even today is much more threatening than most suppose." From the Scriptural standpoint this picture is false, flippant, and fact less. We might well remind ourselves right here that

God reveals himself but the devil conceals himself. He wants to pass off as being something other than he is.

The Bible calls Satan "the god of this world" (II Cor. 4:4). The thorn in my thinking right at this moment is this: This god gets more wealth and worship from his devotees, more fanatical obedience and slavish attention than all the other lesser gods that he has invented (so that they in turn may render homage to him). Do the worshippers of this god of this world tithe? Yes! But they do not tithe with a tenth of what they have—they give him all! Do you know a worldly man who takes his pay packet and carefully selects a tenth of his money to grudgingly hand over for payments of drink, smokes, and gambling?

Are folk clock watchers who take hours to paint and decorate for the ball? When the clock spins past the midnight hour, do they say, "I pray thee have me excused?" No! The fun is only beginning for them at that time. Do Lucifer's children need a stimulant every hour on the hour to get them to see a movie or read the sports page of the paper?

To get men and women to the corner drugstore in order to buy a sordid magazine with an over colored, overstated story of sex, do they have to be mentally clobbered by a suave TV announcer? No! The readers of these sensational mental drugs pass the word along in the factory, or other places. They are actually testifying for the devil.

The children of this world are drunk with generosity at the financial end. Billy Graham stated a while ago that in one afternoon four million dollars were spent at a race track in Florida. According to "Christianity Today" (December 7, 1962), the crime bill in America is a staggering $40,000 a minute. Today it is dollars for death, but dimes for the Word of life! The devil stands as the master brain behind all this Niagara of money that drops into the pit of uselessness. Satan has swapped the sickle of battle for that combined harvester of human flesh, the atom bomb. With his stockpile well-stacked, he would like to trigger off another war that would make all the previous ones look like a backyard skirmish.

In World War I more than 814 million men of battle died. In World War II some 27 million fighting men perished, but our culture allowed us to reach out of the fighting circle and batter helpless civilians so that 25 million of them perished, too. For 52 million people to die in one war is almost too many, one would think. Note with thankfulness that all these died outside of the U.S.A., except for casualties brought in here. Next time, we in the United States shall not get away with that. Satan, I am sure, is restless to fill hell. To him, the end justifies the means. The new atom bomb, we are told, has the potential to wipe out a whole city in less than a minute. Try to think of this as related to New York, London, or Paris.

Add to all this picture of gross folly and human depravity yet another sobering spectacle. The printing presses of the cultists are throbbing night and day as they shake in giving birth to pamphlets and books propagating indoctrinations of seducing spirits and doctrines of devils. Millions of dollars are being spent on temples for false gods. This overall picture is that of a blighting and black situation. The present nervous, needy church has no more chance of stopping this cursed and cruel avalanche than a barrier of straw has of arresting the incoming breakers.

The whole of this nightmarish picture is summarized for us in the Bible phrase, "The whole world lieth in the lap of the evil one."

That is but one-half of the story. The Lord Christ not only delegated His grace to His disciples; He also bequeathed them His power! "I give unto you power... over all the power of the enemy!" To this we have another great promise: "Resist the devil, and he will flee from you." Here we have a clear revelation of the Christian having the whip hand over the devil. The believer is to be the head in this battle and not the tail. Look at these exceeding great and precious promises. (One almost shudders at their magnitude and staggers to think that behind them is the vast, unmeasured wealth and might of the eternal God.)

"Resist the devil, and he will flee from you" (James 4:7).

"Your adversary the devil...whom resist" (I Peter 5:9).

"Whatsoever ye shall bind on earth shall be bound in heaven" (Matt. 18:18).

"Exceeding abundantly...according to the power that worketh in us" (Eph. 3:20).

There are at least three things that we can do with these God-backed promises. The first is to explain them away. The second is to excuse them as the private property of those to whom they were spoken. The third is to expose them and expedite them. If we ignore these Spirit-freighted words, we incur the displeasure of the lord because of our disobedience. Further, we imperil and impoverish our own lives, as well as the lives of others who are led captive by the devil at his will.

Finally, we head for stern censure at the judgment bar of God. The cultist wolves in their sheep's clothing have lured the unlearned into disbelief of the personality of the devil. Their clever brain-washing by twisting Scriptures and speaking lies in hypocrisy, or mocking old-time truth as hell-fire preaching, has had the desired effect of fostering another gospel and adding another fetter to the souls of those already "fast bound in sin and nature's night." Again let me say that the cultist wolves in sheep's clothing have assailed this Bible truth of the personality of the devil and unblushingly traded this perverted view in the vigorous and almost vicious doorstep evangelism. (Why don't believers adopt this method?)

Oh, that the church of the living God would awake and enter into her birthright. "Greater is he that is in (us), than he that is in the world." The path to spiritual victory is clearly shown in the Scriptures: "They overcame him by the blood of the Lamb, and by the word of their testimony" (Rev. 12:11). The blood of Christ is our complete and adequate protection against all the might of the devil.

When Satan fell he drew a third of the heavenly host with him. Therefore, opposing the Christian is the world, the flesh, and the devil, plus one-third of what was the heavenly host. For the Christian are the Father, the Son, the Holy Spirit, and two-thirds of the heavenly host, plus the prayers of many friends and the boundless promises of the unchangeable and indestructible Word of the living God. The balance of power is greatly on the side of the saint. May we so arise from our juvenile Christianity that, armed with the panoply of God and plundering the devil's area, his satanic majesty will have to say, "Jesus I know, and Paul I know, and Christians today are scaring me by discovering a lost secret of the early church- prayer, faith, and blood-covered boldness."

WORLDLY CLERGYMAN

A worldly clergyman is a fool above all fools, a madman above all madmen! Such vile, infamous wretches as these are the real "ground of the contempt of the clergy." Indolent clergymen, pleasure-taking clergymen, money-loving clergymen, praise-loving clergymen, preferment-seeking clergymen—these are the wretches that cause clergymen in general to be contemned. Worldly clergymen are the pest of the Christian world, the grand nuisance of mankind, a stink in the nostrils of God! Such as these were they who made St. Chrysostom say, "Hell is paved with the souls of Christian priests."—Wesley.

Chapter 19

Spirit-Anointed Preaching

CENTURIES have passed since the Swiss reformer Oecolampadius forged the phrase, "How much more would a few good and fervent men affect the ministry than a multitude of lukewarm ones!" The passing of time has not taken the sting from this comparison.

Isaiah had his "Woe of confession"—"Woe is me! for I am undone; because I am a man of unclean lips, and I dwell in the midst of a people of unclean lips." And Paul had his "Woe of commission"—"Woe is unto me if I preach not the gospel!"

Neither of these ordained men had a larger concept of the magnitude of their task than had Richard Baxter of Kidderminister, England. Listen to him in answer to the taunts that he was idle:

"The worst I wish you is that you had my ease instead of your labor. I have reason to take myself for 'the least of all saints,' and yet I fear not to tell 'the accuser' that I take the labor of most tradesmen in the town to be a pleasure to the body in comparison to mine, though I would not exchange it with the greatest prince."

"Their labor preserveth health, and mine consumeth it. They work in ease, and I in continual pain. They have hours and days of recreation; I have scarce time to eat and drink. Nobody molesteth them for their labor, but the more I do, the more hatred and trouble I draw upon me."

There is something of New Testament soul culture about that attitude to preaching. This is the Baxter who ever sought to preach as a dying man to dying men. A generation of preachers of his soul caliber would rescue this generation of sinners from the greedy mouth of a yawning hell.

We may have an all-time high in church attendance with a corresponding all-time low in spirituality. Liberalism was cursed by many as the seducer of the people. Now TV is the scapegoat, getting the anathema of the preachers.

Having said that, and knowing that both indictments carry truth, may I ask a question? Have we preachers to confess with one of old, "The fault, dear Brutus, is within ourselves"?

To sharpen my scalpel and plunge it into the quivering flesh of us pulpiteers—Has great preaching died? Is soul-hot preaching a lost art? Have we conceded to the impatient modern snack-bar sermons, spiced with humor to edge jaded spiritual appetites? Do we endeavor to bring the "power of the world to come" into every meeting?

With a powerful anointing of the Holy Spirit upon him, Paul went out to ransack Asia Minor, mauling its markets, stirring its synagogues, penetrating its palaces. Out he went, with the war cry of the gospel in his heart and on his lips.

Lenin is credited with coining the phrase, "Facts are stubborn things." How right he was! Look at the achievements of this man Paul, and sicken at the compromise of this generation of Christians! Paul was not merely a city-wide preacher, but a city-wide shaker. Yet he had time to knock on the doors along the street and pray for lost souls in the street.

The playboys of yesterday are the payboys of evangelism. A top-line evangelist of my knowledge actually refused a contract of five hundred dollars a week for a four weeks' preaching campaign. No wonder a modernist has declared that these evangelists will weep for souls—if the price is right! Aye, like Judas, they will be weeping when it is too late. Weakness in the pew may be because of wickedness in the pulpit.

I am increasingly convinced that tears are an integral part of revival preaching. Preacher brethren, this is the time to blush that we have no shame, the time to weep for our lack of tears, the time to bend low that we have lost the humble touch of servants, the time to groan that we have no burden, the time to be angry with ourselves that we have no anger over the devil's monopoly in this end-time hour, the time to chastise ourselves that the world can get along with us as easily and not attempt to chastise us.

YOU-ENDUED AS Peter

Pentecost meant pain, and we have so much pleasure. Pentecost meant burden, and we love ease. Pentecost meant prison, and most of us would do anything rather than get there for Christ's dear sake. Pentecost re-lived would get many of us in jail.

Imagine Pentecost in your church this Sunday—YOU endued as was Peter, and under your word, brother Ananias is slain and his wife soon stiff beside him! Would the moderns stand for that?

Here is a Paul smiting Elymas with blindness. That would bring a court case against any preacher these days. Even prostration (that has accompanied almost all revival preaching) would get us a bad name, and that is more than our tender hearts could take.

I am appealing again, as at the beginning of this article, for majestic preaching. The devil wants us to major on minors. Read an article today on dress. I am all for sobriety. But many of us in the deeper life bracket are hunting mice while lions devour the land!

What happened to Paul while in Arabia, I have never been able to find out. No one knows. Did he get a glimpse of the new heaven and the new earth and see the exalted Lord reigning over all? I still do not know. But this much is sure: he altered Asia, jaundiced the Jews, riled the Romans, taught the teachers, and pitied prison jailers. This man Paul and another preacher called Silas dynamited prison walls-with prayer-and cost the tax payers a load in order that they might get about the Master's business.

Having settled that he himself was the hardest soul that God would ever have to deal with, Paul the bond-slave, Paul the love-slave, strode out to shake regions for God. He brought the powers of the world to come on his day, stayed Satan, and outsuffered, outloved, and outprayed us all.

Brethren, to our knees again-to rediscover apostolic piety and apostolic power. Away with sickly sermonizing!

Chapter 20

A Man After
God's Own Heart

WHEN THIS presbytery was held, outside the memory of most of us, the church in Cumberland was troubled and in crisis. "The love of many (had waxed) cold." Defections had occurred. Some of the masters in her Israel had withdrawn, carrying off weight and influence and leaving behind them a host of perplexed people. The future of this assembly was shrouded in darkness. Some members were threatening to dissolve the church-unless there were revolutionary changes made both in doctrine and in policy.

The apex of this dissipation in spiritual power was shown markedly in the absence of candidates for the ministry.

The members of the semi-annual convocation were veterans—mostly weather beaten veterans. They had wrestled on 'gainst wind and storm and tide." Neither blinding snowstorms nor torrid heat had kept them from long horse riding in order to deliver "the whole counsel of God." With their fighting hearts but failing bodies, it was hard for them to understand why this younger generation of men could "eat their morsel alone."

The presbytery was held in candlelight in a member's large log cabin, and it was exceptionally full. On that now- historic cabin was to fall the Glory held in "earthen vessels." This special meeting had been called to test young men and seek those (if such there were) who would volunteer for the ministry. On such an occasion many a man, now well-accepted in his denomination as a burning and shining light, could tell of his awkwardness and unpromising exhibition. This time was to be no exception.

At the call of the presiding officer to "all who had felt impressions to preach to come forward and converse with the presbytery on the subject," three men stepped before the packed house. Of the first two we shall not speak. The third man had stood partly concealed in a dark corner of the room while the other candidates spoke. He now stepped forward.

His appearance excited a universal gasp of surprise even in that unsophisticated audience accustomed as they were to rudeness of dress and uncouth manners.

Get this picture if you can. Imagine this tall mountain boy, dressed in copperas cloth-that is, a cloth homespun, home-woven, home-cut, and home-sewed, dyed in that bilious hue which is formed by copperas, alum, and walnut bark, and made into a clumsy coat, vest and breeches. To this, add brogans of home-tanned, red leather, tied with a leather thong and covering immense feet (both feet and brogans were made for climbing hills). Now you have the portrait of this mountain boy. He could live off his rifle and whip any lowland boy in the state.

150

This is the angular lad who stepped from the dark of the corner into the blinking light of the candles and pine-log fire. He was weeping bitterly, and, having no such thing as a handkerchief, he adopted the original arrangement provided for such emergency. For a full minute he stood silent, every curious eye fastened upon him, every agitated mind wondering what on earth he would announce as his business. He cleared his throat, then commenced: "I've come to Presby—." But a new wave of tears stopped his utterance.

The moderator kindly prompted, "You came here why, my son? Take your time, tell us all about it; none here will hurt you."

As the storm in his soul prevailed, the stranger started again, and yet again, and then a fourth time. Only to be choked with his own tears. Some good brother suggested that the young man be interviewed privately. The mountain lad demurred at this, replying that he'd "get my voice d'reckly, please God." And so he did, and rose up, straightening his gaunt, awkward frame.

Then such words flowed from his lips that surpassed anything that had ever rung through that assembly. We shall not attempt to report the address. Enough to say that the oldest minister there said that his words scorched and burnt wherever they fell. The alarm in that rugged boy's soul swept through the whole place. This was his story.

A few months before, he had fallen in with a traveling preacher who had gotten lost on the thin mountain tracks. The minister, interested in the odd appearance of the boy and gripped by his total ignorance of things spiritual, had given him one whole hour of his precious time to telling of the sin of the world and the lost estate of the boy. The talk concluded with the godly man kneeling at the root of a tree and earnestly pouring out his heart's desire for the unenlightened soul. Days later the boy heard an inward voice saying, "Repent, repent; why will ye die?" A weight like a mountain weighed down upon his soul. Sleep forsook his eyelids. His axe rusted by the pile. His rifle hung dust-covered on the wall.

The simple-hearted neighbors, ignorant as the boy himself, pronounced him deranged. The younger fry twitted him that he was in love. Some whispered behind their hands that it might be liquor. Despite visiting some preaching houses, he received no help but continued seeking. In many churches they now remember the apparition of the ill-clad youth sitting well up on the front seat, listening with ears and mouth with the attention that a man ready for the gallows would give at the sight of the distant horseman who, perhaps, brings him an expected reprieve.

In a camp meeting the place was shattered when the lad first saw the light. His happy cry, "I've got it! I've got it" electrified his own breast and made others weep for joy. With the speed of Jehu, he went home to tell the neighbors what the Lord had done for his soul. Forsaking all other duties, he went from cabin to cabin in the exultant joy of the spiritual new birth. Daily his ardor increased. In amazement the mountaineers listened to their John Baptist as he called them

A MAN AFTER GOD'S OWN HEART to forsake sin and call on the name of the Lord.

By the time this moved and moving man had finished his spell-binding oration to the presbytery, the pine fire had burned low; the dipped and shapeless candles had melted themselves down. His language in parts was as uncouth as that of a bush native. His gestures were stiff. He alternated between crying and laughing as he wandered from his broken agony to his final triumph, shouting until his voice boomed back from the hillside as he enchained the heart of every listener. The gray-haired moderator sobbed aloud. From time to time the excitable joined in with the preacher's loud amen. The presbyters met, talked, decided that none could withhold a preacher's license from him. George Willets was duly received as a candidate for the ministry.

Ten years later this rough lad was still a fireball, still tireless in seeking the lost, still praying without ceasing, a clerical lion, fearless, strong-and yet tender with the compassion of his Lord. When he talked of heaven, men felt they were in the vestibule of the city of God. When he spoke of hell-and it was with tenderness as well as terror-men trembled.

He descanted on the terrors of the damned until every shuddering face turned downward as if to see the solid globe rent asunder and the smoke of the bottomless pit billowing up. Strong men moaned like infants; ladies in silk shrieked as if a knife were plunged into them.

He reflected on "the city that hath foundations whose builder and maker is God." He pointed with a sharp finger at the sky as if the parting clouds offered a chink through which men could creep to the feet of a pardoning God. So stirring and heart-born was the word that almost all gazed into heaven to look for mercy. He then called mourners to the altar. On one occasion more than five hundred went forward, smitten with the sword of the Spirit.

George Willets' dress and manner are not to be copied by the preacher of this hour. But unless we are baptized with the same compassion, icicles will soon be hanging from our pulpits.

Part Two

Portraits of
Revival Preachers

George Fox

"Above all, George Fox excelled in prayer. The inwardness and weight of his spirit, the reverence and solemnity of his address and behavior, and the fewness and fullness of his words have often struck even strangers with admiration as they used to reach others with consolation. The most awful, living, reverend frame I ever felt or beheld, I must say, was the prayer of George Fox. And truly it was a testimony. He knew and lived nearer to the Lord than other men, for they that know Him most will see most reason to approach Him with reverence and fear."

—By William Penn

Chapter 21

George Fox
The Unshakable Shaker

1624-1691

"THE MOST remarkable incident in modern history perhaps is not the Diet of Worms, still less the battle of Austerlitz or Peterloo, or any other battle.

"The most remarkable incident is passed over carelessly by most historians and treated with some degree of ridicule by others-namely, George Fox's making for himself a suit of leather.

"No grander thing was ever done than when George Fox, stitching himself into a suit of leather, went forth determined to find truth for himself-and to do battle for it against all superstition and intolerance."

This was Thomas Carlyle's considered opinion about the poor, uneducated English shoemaker, George Fox. So hard was his itinerate preaching life that he made for himself that famous pair of leather breeches, which have since become historical. Those breeches were known all over the country, says Macauley the historian. In the middle of the seventeenth century men feared the man dressed in that famous suit as much as the Jordan spectators, centuries before, feared the man who had the leathern girdle about his loins and who ate locusts and wild honey. And rightly so, for George Fox and John the Baptist were kindred spirits.

George Fox first saw the light of day in 1624 at Drayton-in-the-Clay, Leicestershire, England. His Godly parents belonged to the Church of England and endeavored to bring up their children in the fear of the Lord. George's first step in his long quest for spirituality was at the age of eleven when he surrendered his heart to the Lord. Ever after, he sought to live an honest and upright life.

The Reformation fires of one hundred years before had burned themselves out. Among the clergy there abounded much education, loose-living, and ease. The Protestant church had a name to live but was dead.

George Fox did not enjoy any personal direct communion with God until he was nineteen. Then for some time his soul was full of strange longings and continual Teachings out after God. The Christians he met did not possess what they professed. So deeply was he grieved and distressed over examples of their hypocrisy that he could not sleep all night but walked up and down in his room praying to God. He sought help from man but found none.

His relatives did not know what to make of George. One kind soul said that marriage was the remedy for his melancholic state of mind. Another proffered the view that he should enlist in the army. A third believed the use of tobacco and singing psalms would bring relief.

No wonder the seeking soul thought that his advisers were all "miserable comforters." One man, supposedly experienced in the things of God, was "like an empty hollow cask" to George Fox. Seeking the advice of a clergyman, Fox accidentally stepped on the minister's flower bed, whereupon the angry cleric flew into a rage.

Finding no help from men. Fox gave up seeking from that source. With the Bible as his guide, he began looking to the Lord alone for help. Slowly the light began to dawn upon him. He was led to see that only those who had passed from death to life were real believers in Christ. Once and for all Fox settled it that "being bred at Oxford and Cambridge did not qualify or fit a man to be a minister of Christ."

When George Fox was about 23, he began preaching to others the truths revealed to him. He was mightily used of God. Thus he came in the nick of time "to save the church from deadness and formalism, and the world from infidelity." He was sent of God to call the church to real spiritual worship.

Fox began his preaching with a limited education, without any special training, and without special advantages of any kind. He so preached that men got the shakes. The name Quaker was attached to Fox and his followers because of the quaking of the men who came to scoff but stayed to pray. Though he made others shake, no man living could make him shake.

Walking bare-footed through the crowded market at Litchfield, England, this man in the leather suit upraised his hands and voice, shouting, "Woe unto Litchfield, thou bloody city! Woe unto Litchfield!" He feared neither man nor the consequences of his tirade. At first the crowd was amused, then serious, then terrified.

Here was a man with unquenchable zeal. He had "heard a voice." Beat him they might, cast him into prison they would, mock him as a madman they laughingly did. But still he proclaimed the message of Christ. Shut out of churches, George Fox made a stone his pulpit and preached to the crowds in the streets. Taken from the street meeting to the jail, he made the jail a cathedral to declare the wonderful works of God. Often he was found praising the Lord in a stinking prison cell.

From judge to criminal, from Lord Protector to kitchen maid. Fox bore a burning witness. "He itinerated the British Isles," says one of his biographers, "preaching and protesting as no man before him had ever done. In his preaching he wore out clothes, horses, critics, persecutors, and eventually himself."

Many times Fox prophesied of future events that were revealed to him. Visions often came to him. Once in Lancashire, England, as he was climbing Pendle Hill, he had a vision of a coming revival in that very area. He "saw the countryside alive with men, all moving to one place." I have worshipped in the old mullion-windowed meeting house erected after the great visitation of God in that area.

In personal appearance Fox was a large man with remarkable piercing eyes. His words were like a flash of lightning. His judgment was clear, and his logic convincing. His great spiritual gift was a remarkable discernment. He seemed to be able to read the characters of men by looking at them. He likened the temperaments of people to a wolf, a serpent, a lion, or a wasp. He could meet a person and say, "I see the spirit of a cunning fox in you." "You have the nature of a serpent." Or "Thou art as vicious as a tiger." Fox was far in advance of any other person in his day, in spiritual matters.

"Above all, George Fox excelled in prayer."

The great secret of Fox's power was his faith in God. He started with scarcely any advantages, but soon he influenced the whole world for God. His one desire was the extension of Christ's kingdom on earth. Through his influence England, Ireland, and Scotland were soon ablaze. In 1661 several of, his followers were moved to go beyond the seas to publish truth in foreign countries. In 1664 he married Margaret Fell. In 1670-73 he sailed for the West Indies and North America. Though he was persecuted even there, the work spread.

No religious or political reformer was ever imprisoned as many times as George Fox, and oh, what prisons! But his times in prison were missionary labors. Not in solitary confinement, he always had a congregation. But he made converts. His fame spread and people came in crowds to hear him.

A distinguished American governor, Livingston, was justified in giving the following elevated opinion of "the unshakable shaker":

George Fox alone has, without human learning, done more than any other reformer in Protestant Christendom towards the restoration of real, primitive, unadulterated—Christianity, and the destruction of priest-craft, superstition, and ridiculous, unavailing rites and ceremonies.

He left us an example of fearless, devoted service that alas, but few have ever tried to follow. "He saw hell and heaven, God and judgment with such a clear vision that he was forced to go out in season and out of season to snatch poor sinners from their awful doom. Constantly he appeared just where nobody expected him, blocking the road to hell and pointing the road to heaven—and all because he was completely delivered from all regard for public opinion and utterly impatient of useless routine."

How cities throughout the world today could be made to quake by workers as full of God and faith, as reckless as to their life and interest and comfort, as determined to wreck the devil's kingdom as George Fox was!

Once Fox grasped the truth that he sought for, there was a steady calm in his spiritual life. There were no ups and downs; his life was pure and childlike and truly hid with Christ in God.

His preaching was plain but powerful. It may have lacked eloquence or clearness, it may have been given in involved sentences and been almost unintelligible, but the Holy Ghost was never lacking in all of Fox's discourses. He excelled in prayer.

The work by which Fox is principally known is "Fox's Journal." This book, which was printed three years after his death, is one of the world's most famous books, "rich in spiritual insight, in noble simplicity and in moral fibre." It was Fox's presence and spoken words which made the deep impression vividly portrayed in his journal.

George Fox died in London, January 13, 1691. If you are ever in London, go to his grave right opposite John Wesley's church in City Road in the weary-looking Bunhill Field. Despite its moss and age, you will read on the leaning tombstone, "Here lies George Fox!" He is in good company, for beside him, waiting for the great day, sleep Wesley's mother, Susannah, Isaac Watts, Daniel Defoe, and other famed folk. George Fox, who honored the Son, will one day be honored by Him. Sleep on, faithful, fighting Fox!

Chapter 22

William Grimshaw of Haworth

IT WAS an unusual coffin and occupied by an unusual preacher. The deceased who lay in it had left specifications: it must be cheap, very plain, painted, and then clearly lettered with his favorite text—"To me to live is Christ, and to die is gain" (Phil. 1:21).

In that coffin in Haworth, England, lay the mortal remains of William Grimshaw—a circuit rider before Wesley ever thought of circuit riders. Here lay a man who pre-dated John Wesley in establishing class meetings.

At this funeral in June, 1763, the great crowd lamented the passing of their minister. The oration was made by Henry Venn, the famed author of "The Complete Duty of Man." He cried.

"Witness, ye mountains and moors, how often Grimshaw was 'in perils by the way' whilst carrying the glad tidings of salvation to some poor cottager who, but for Grimshaw's instruction, would have died as ignorant of Christ as when he was born.

"Witness, ye stormy rains and piercing cold of winter, ye fainting sultry clouds of summer, how many seasons Grimshaw exposed himself to your inclemencies, if by any means he might save some. No roads were too dangerous in his work, no refreshment too coarse, no lodging too hard, no discouragement too great. His work of itself was his wages and as much as he desired."

We know comparatively little about Grimshaw's early life. He was born in Lancaster County, England, where many of the churches at that time were as barren of spiritual power as the moorland rocks were of vegetation. He seems to have been moved by religious feelings early. In 1720 his parents sent him to Cambridge to receive instruction for the ministry. There he seems to have fallen into loose company and learned to drink and swear. In 1731 he returned to Lancashire and became curate of Rochdale Parish Church. Upon his ordination his rector gave him Brooks' "Precious Remedies Against Satan's Devices."

For a while this book aroused in him a fleeting glimpse of the importance of his office and sobered him. As a typical parson, he was content to do his Sunday duty by "saying services" and reading a sermon to the congregation. Later he seems to have slipped back rapidly into his Cambridge ways, an "easy companion for easy men."

In 1734 Grimshaw himself changed his ways and became serious. Prevenient grace worked in him, and he had what the old Quakers would have called "a concern." Because of this, he dropped his card playing, hunting, and drinking, and began the custom of praying four times a day. He kept this custom. says Henry Venn, until he died.

But this was not Grimshaw's conversion. He simply had conviction of guilt and knew that his goodness could not procure him pardon. This period of self-stripping from wicked works and habits left him still unsatisfied. After five years of great happiness in marriage, his wife died, leaving him to care for two children. The blow was profound.

By this time Grimshaw had a conception of the omnipotence of God but none of His power to forgive. He knew his life was useless but knew not as yet where to turn for power. His sermons were pleas to renounce sin before the wrath of God, but he knew not the source of power over sin.

In 1742, eight years after his awakening, the cloud lifted suddenly, and Grimshaw found peace with God. He testified that after he had known regeneration, the Bible seemed as if it had been drawn up to heaven and a new one sent down.

John Newton (1725-1807) is without doubt the best biographer of Grimshaw. He reveals through his letters that after his crisis experience with God, Grimshaw's preaching became clear and profitable. He wrote to the distinguished preacher Henry Venn: "I am now willing to renounce myself, every degree of fancied merit and ability, and to embrace Christ for my all in all. Oh what light and comfort I now enjoy in my soul! What a state of the pardoning love of God."

In June of that same year, right in the middle of the great period of revival in church history (1714-1800),

Grimshaw was appointed to Haworth. (This is where the famed novelist Bronte sisters-Charlotte, Emily and Anna-made their sojourn in the rectory.) Here he was to minister for twenty-one years.

Haworth, a hamlet of 2,600, was bleak and wet. At first there were only twelve communicants. More beer was consumed than in most places. The Church of England was decadent. Some even thought that Christ had been discovered to be fictitious. But the Lord was pleased to visit the parish. The church began to be crowded, insomuch that many were obliged to stand out of doors. Men were seized with weeping, roaring, and agonies at the fear of their sinful state and wrath of God. Grimshaw's preaching was attracting crowds.

Then Grimshaw started touring his wide parish and preaching twelve times a month in cottages in each of its four scattered hamlets. Gradually he began to itinerate, going outside his own parish to speak in cottage meetings. Converted before meeting the Wesleys (and after reading only one sermon by a Methodist), Grimshaw was itinerating like the Methodists and joining his converts in classes even before he met John and Charles Wesley in 1742.

He transformed the parish and the district around by his apostolic activities, his life of constant prayer, and his ceaseless devotion to the public worship of the church he loved and served. In seven years' time he had a congregation of 300 to 400 in the winter, and 1,000 to 1,200 in summer—besides his twelve meetings in the hamlets of his parish each month of the year.

At this time, that is during the first half of the eighteenth century, England was in a state of religious and moral decay. The land had been sinking into darkness and paganism for many years. Increasingly the characteristics of the age were intemperance and immorality, crime and cruelty.

But there came an awakening in the church. In Grimshaw's day God seemed to have furnished a whole Milky Way of preachers, though one star differed from another star in glory. The young flaming George Whitefield (1714-1770) was stirring the silk-gowned ladies, as well as making the miners weep. On one of his visits to Haworth, the great orator took as his text, "It is appointed unto men once to die, and after that the judgment." While he was speaking, a man actually died.

The secret of Grimshaw's influence and power can largely be attributed to three things: He knew himself to be called and sent by God. Such knowledge gave him inspiration, courage, and zeal. Moreover, he knew the message that he was sent to deliver, the clear, definite gospel of the redeeming love of Christ, crucified and risen, was ever before him: "Woe is unto me, if I preach not the gospel!" (I Corinthians 9:16).

Lastly, he had a great love for souls. His love was a fever with him so that his preaching flowed from a volcanic heart with holy ease. In his "lazy week" he preached fourteen times; in his normal week, twenty or thirty times. On one occasion he apologized to a sick lady for his absence from sick visitation, explaining that he had preached no less than thirty times that week. Many of these meetings were in the market places where the people gathered to buy and sell produce. One of his converts came to be instrumental in sending William Carey to Serampore.

The key to Grimshaw's great soul-winning was prayer. Sunday mornings he would often rise before five. As we have said, in 1734 he began a lifetime habit of praying four times a day. He prayed as he dressed. He prayed with his family. He prayed before and after meals (blessing God for the benefit of them). He prayed as he worked. He prayed in the evening.

In his pursuit of souls, he would disguise himself and go out on a Sunday to the boys who went to gamble on the hills. There he would find out their names and entreat them to come to see him at his home. In this way some were led to the Lord. It was his custom before church services to fetch the men from the four alehouses within a child's stone-throw of the church and bring them in.

He rebuked sin in private or in public. Great men and small were in danger of hell—eternal hell. He would save some at all costs. As he yearned over the impiety of the stouthearted, roughly crusted with sin, often he would weep. His compassionate interceding with God for men and then with men for God was a tonic to a sick church.

Humility was a shining virtue with Grimshaw. When he had guests, it was his custom to be up early, cleaning their boots. Sometimes when his house was full of visiting preachers, he himself would slip out and sleep in the hay-loft.

Time would fail me to tell of Grimshaw's fiery trials, his zeal for souls, his care for the widows, his generosity to other preachers. But the fastings he kept (and they were often), the tears he shed (and they were many), the souls he won (and there were hundreds)-are these not all recorded in the book of the chronicles at the Throne of God?

Grimshaw died a poor man in 1763. His memorial lay not in riches but in countless Christians. Through his preaching, early and late, their lives had been remade in Christ. The town of Haworth changed during his ministry. "Never was any sordid child of the world more engrossed by the love of money and more laborious in heaping it up than William Grimshaw was in teaching and preaching the kingdom of God and the things concerning the Lord Jesus Christ." Grimshaw would certainly have approved Venn's funeral remarks: "Worthy is the Lamb that was slain to receive power, and riches, and honor and glory and blessing."

Within fifty years of his death, William Grimshaw, once called the Apostle of the North, was the subject of four biographies. Our generation has almost completely forgotten Grimshaw's life; or if he is known at all, he is remembered not for the devotion and humility which impressed his contemporaries but as the man who fetched his congregation from the alehouse with a horsewhip.

In recent years we have ignored the contribution of the Evangelical Revival to the eighteenth century. As Lecky has written, "The great evangelicals of the eighteenth century- Grimshaw included—gradually changed the whole spirit of the church in England. They infused into it a new fire and passion of devotion, kindled a spirit of fervent philanthropy, raised the standard of clerical duty, and completely altered the whole tone and tendency of the preaching of the ministers.'

There is a famine of good preaching right now. The hungry sheep look up and are not fed."

Chapter 23

Jonathan Edwards

READ closely this study in a series of pen portraits of men whom God has used as channels for revival in the Christian religion. The vocabularies of these men were as different as their dress. Their backgrounds were of contrasting variety. Their moods and expressions were as unrelated as the limits of human personality could make them. Yet they were one—one because like Moses they "endured as seeing him who is invisible." They bent their every power and talent to turn men from darkness to light and from the power of Satan unto God. These men have been the foundation stones of the generations.

Yet who among us sees or appreciates foundation stones? At a sky-clutching tower of a new building or at a slender finger of stones for the church spire, we will gaze and gaze. But who pauses often to think of the rough foundation stones buried in the cold, wet, dirty earth? Biographies are so fallible and often are incomplete. God alone knows all men's tears and their travails. The "great day" alone will give the full score.

Down the history of the church there have been a few Jonathan-David knit-together souls. Such combinations are full of luster because they are so infrequent and they have been so purged of self-promotion that they often appear to us to be the figment of a poet's imagination.

However we do not find many of these dual laborers. The leaders of revival periods whom we are about to sketch have often been lonely souls. They were well-known once, or we would not have considered them as candidates for this selection. But today they are not well-known. In our day many of these men who "tasted the powers of the world to come" would be sidelined, for our emphasis seems to be on platform talent and public appeal. Yet I am sure each portrait can teach us something in soul devotion and soul passion.

Today, so much of what we "put over" in evangelism is sensory and not spiritual. The day of cowbell gospel entertainment should never have been born. (I pray God it may soon die.) Never for a split second would Paul the apostle have dreamed that evangelism could have become an industry, or tithing be operated and encouraged on a Wall Street basis. On the contrary, these men have been sketched in words, they

"Climbed the steep ascent to heaven
Through peril, toil, and pain.
O God, to us may grace be given
To follow in their train!"

Jonathan Edwards, 1703-1758, achieved greatness as an American preacher-evangelist, principal of a college, mystic, and revivalist.

"Jonathan Edwards is not only the greatest of all American theologians and philosophers but the greatest of our pre-19th century writers as well." So writes Randall Stewart in his book American Literature and Christian Doctrine."

Here is a concise summary of the life of Edwards from the able pen of Perry Miller: "Jonathan Edwards was one of America's five or six major artists—who happened to work with ideas instead of with poems or novels. He was much more of a psychologist and poet than a logician. Though he devoted his genius to topics derived from the body of divinity (the will, virtue, sin), he traced them in the manner of the very finest spectator..."

For us to see Jonathan Edwards ascend his pulpit today, a candle in one hand and his sermon manuscript in the other, would cause a titter in the congregation. From our modern foam-cushioned church seats, with carpeted aisles and soothing background music, we can scarcely capture the old- time dignity of the unpretentious church where Edwards and others held captive the hearts and minds of their hearers.

When Jonathan Edwards "uttered" in the Spirit, the expressionless face, the sonorous voice, the sober clothing were forgotten. He was neither a dullard nor a sluggard. His was a devoted heart intent on rightly dividing the word of truth. But in doing it, Edwards flamed. Yet to him, sensationalism was anathema. To make an impression was never the thought behind any of his preaching. Scholarship on fire for God is to my mind the eighth wonder of the world. Edwards had it.

The tongue of Edwards must have been like a sharp two-edged sword to his attentive hearers. His words must have been as painful to their hearts and consciences as burning metal on flesh. Nevertheless, men gave heed, repented, and were saved.

"Knowing the terror of the Lord" (a thing seemingly forgotten in our day both by pulpit and pew), Edwards smoldered with holy wrath. Impervious to any consequences of such severity, he thundered these words from his pulpit:

"The bow of God's wrath is bent, and His arrows made ready upon the string. Justice points the arrow at your heart and strings the bow. It is nothing but the mere pleasure of God (and that of an angry God without any promise or obligation at all) that keeps the arrow one moment from being made drunk with your blood."

To utter truth like that with tears and tenderness takes an anointed and therefore fearless and compassionate man.

But in the hearts and minds of the hearers there must also have been some prevenient grace at work. Apart from this, men would have rebelled at this stern sweep of power on their souls. As it was, before Edwards' spiritual hurricane, the crowd collapsed. Some fell to the earth as if pole-axed. Others, with heads bowed, clung onto the posts of the temple as if afraid of falling into the nethermost depths of hell.

Edwards wept as he preached. In this he was a kinsman in soul of the mighty Brownlow North of the revival that occurred years later in Ireland in 1859. The divine law of Psalm 126:6 never has nor ever can be abrogated: "He that goeth forth and weepeth, bearing precious seed, shall doubtless come again with rejoicing, bringing his sheaves with him."

As pastor of one of New England's largest, wealthiest, and most socially-conscious congregations, Edwards had a rare perception of the needs of his flock. He also had a heart of great tenderness for their spiritual health.

Let's go to the woods where Edwards is alone with his God. Let's creep up behind that old gnarled tree and listen to his broken prayer:

"I feel an urgency of soul to be…emptied and annihilated, to lie in the dust and be full of Christ alone, to love Him with a holy and pure love, to trust in Him, to live on Him, and to be perfectly sanctified and made pure with a divine and heavenly purity."

Edwards was also a soul kinsman of George Whitefield, his contemporary. Was the mighty American, Jonathan Edwards, sparked by the English apostle, Whitefield? Did the thunderings from the vibrant soul of Whitefield, then storming through New England, disturb and challenge the normality of Edwards' preaching life? This is not a rhetorical question. It cannot be answered fully, but it contains more than a grain of truth. We do know that after meeting young George Whitefield, Jonathan Edwards changed his style of sermon notes.

It pleased the Lord to sideline Edwards to a small pastorate at Stockbridge, Mass. This banishment came because of his difference with a Mr. Stoddard, who had administered the Lord's Supper to some who had not made public confession of their faith in Jesus Christ as their personal Savior. But in his seclusion, Edwards' brilliant mind took wings. His long-incubated thinking came to the birth. Thus he might have said to Mr. Stoddard what Joseph said to his brethren: "Ye meant evil against me; but God meant it for good." The Lord again turned the wrath of man to praise Him for at this time Edwards' soul got the measure of "words." From his pen flowed the best of his writings. Edwards sleeps, but his message still speaks.

When the voice of Milton had long been silenced by death, Wordsworth cried,

> Milton, thou should'st be living at this hour:
> England hath need of thee;
> She is a fen of stagnant waters.

We could paraphrase those words thus:

> Edwards, thou should'st be living at this hour:
> America hath need of thee:
> She is a fen (spiritually) of stagnant waters.

A thin crust, a very thin crust of morality, it seems to me, keeps America from complete collapse. In this perilous hour we need a whole generation of preachers like Edwards.

"O Lord of hosts, turn us again; cause Thy face to shine upon us, and we shall be saved."

Contrast this great man of God with his contemporary, quote from Al Sanders in "Crisis in Morality!"

"Max Jukes, the atheist, lived a godless life. He married an ungodly girl, and from the union there were 310 who died as paupers, 150 were criminals, 7 were murderers, 100 were drunkards, and more than half of the women were prostitutes. His 540 descendants cost the State one and a quarter million dollars.

"But, praise the Lord, it works both ways! There is a record of a great American man of God, Jonathan Edwards. He lived at the same time as Max Jukes, but he married a godly girl. An investigation was made of 1,394 known descendants of Jonathan Edwards of which 13 became college presidents, 65 college professors, 3 United States senators, 30 judges, 100 lawyers, 60 physicians, 75 army and navy officers, 100 preachers and missionaries, 60 authors of prominence, one a vice-president of the United States, 80 became public officials in other capacities, 295 college graduates, among whom were governors of states and ministers to foreign countries. His descendants did not cost the state a single penny. The memory of the just is blessed' (Prov. 10:7)."

To us this is the conclusion of the whole matter.

Chapter 24

Gideon Ousely

The Irish Wesley 1762-1841

IN 1762 John Wesley made his second invasion of the City of Galway in Ireland. Unknown to him, snug in his cradle in a corner of the same country lay a baby boy who, when Wesley had ceased his labors, would be beginning a ministry scarcely less effective and endued with the same baptism of fire. Gideon Ousely, for that was the name of this God-endued soul winner, was born in Dunmore, Ireland, on February 24, 1762.

His mother was careful to safeguard Gideon from his father's ideas on Deism. She had the boy read to her at nights from Tillotson's "Sermons" or Young's "Night Thoughts" and his "Last Day." Time did not erase these thoughts from the mind of the reader.

Gideon was first awakened to his lost estate by a man who was a soldier fighting in two armies at the same time—the Fourth Royal Irish Dragoon Guards and the army of the Lord.

He was also deeply affected by the preaching of John Hurley and under his anointed exhortation he came into grace. In his twenty-ninth year in the middle of May,

1791, Gideon beheld "the Lamb of God slain for him" and felt that God had taken the load and darkness away and had bestowed the long-sought peace.

At the "Class meeting" John Hurley asked him, "Do you believe that the Lord has pardoned you?"

"Yes," he replied, "my soul doth magnify the Lord, and my spirit doth rejoice in God my Savior."

Later, over the Irish countryside, as dumb beasts would look over the fences, they heard the singing soul of the horse-borne preacher, eloquent and loud in his praises to the One who, as Wesley put it, "Saved poor souls out of the fire and quenched their brands in Jesus' blood."

The Irish preacher of whom I write had but one eye. Yet no man with two eyes ever saw more clearly from the divine record that men are lost now and lost forever except they repent, than did this man. Men to him were not men, but spirits wrapped in flesh—souls for whom Christ died. He saw them as potential jewels for the diadem of Christ or fuel for the flames of hell.

Sparks flew from the hoofs of his flying horse with its foam-trimmed mouth and sweating flanks as he sped with pitiful urgency on those rough Irish roads. One would think that this preacher had had a preview of hell or a secret note delivered by Gabriel himself that the end of the age would come within the next twenty-four hours. Such was his quenchless zeal for souls. There can be no doubt about it that this blessed man could say, "The zeal of thine house hath eaten me up."

Neither Paul Revere of America or John Gilpin of England ever rode with more zeal than this "Irish Wesley" as some have called him. It might be nearer the mark to class him with England's Whitefield or America's Gilbert Tennent. He was their kinsman in spirit. He belonged to the fellowship which leaps ecclesiastical labels-the fellowship of the burning heart.

In London, St. Paul's Cathedral has a pulpit in impressive marble. In this City Road Chapel, Wesley had a nice polished mahogany pulpit. Jesus used the rim of a well for a pulpit. Our hero had for his pulpit often times a pair of stirrups or a backless saddle.

Consider the scope of one of Ousley's prayer-baptized missionary journeys among the unlettered Irish folk of the then wild countryside. See these things happen. A priest stands waiting for the wedding party to enter the church. When the carriage bringing the happy couple arrives, our hero preacher walks to them. He gently warns them of eternity, and, in a few minutes, the happy couple are startled to find themselves involuntarily kneeling on the ground while the flaming evangelist prays for them. He then rushes on. Over the cemetery wall he espies weeping souls, wailing and affrighted because their loved one has gone-whither? He lifts his great voice in prayer above their flesh-freezing cries.

Next see Ousely in the market place. This is the scene of a last public execution. Thousands are gathered. I believe it was our preacher who climbed the scaffold and ministered to the shaking criminal. After he had led the man to Christ, the preacher with the scaffold for a pulpit, bombarded the crowd with the facts of eternal solemnity. As he spoke, the body of the dead was swinging from the scaffold. Within sight of death he preached to the careless sinners of eternal life. As he pictured for them the eternal woes of those who die without God and without hope, he turned their dancing into mourning.

One who heard Ousely testify said later, "I wish I could reproduce his testimony as I heard it. The solemnity and loving earnestness of his manner, the melting tone of his voice, the beaming look, the grateful joy, the flowing tears, the impassioned character of his appeals, cannot be reproduced on paper."

Gideon took more than one preaching tour of England. There, as in Ireland, he saw the manifest power of the Lord, evidenced not only in striking conversions, but also in phenomena. Folk would fall into a swoon while he preached. Some would appear to be dead and respond neither to gentle attention nor to shouting and shaking. Later they "awoke" and entered into the peace of salvation.

The flaming soul was driven from market place and derided from pulpit. Priests and Protestant alike sought to put road blocks in the way of this advancing crusader. On he pushed.

His spirit was willing, though at times his flesh was weak. But he drove it on. Rough riding, rough eating, rough sleeping, and rough crowds in the markets all made draining demands upon him. Yet in his 75th year he was still street preaching and holding the attention of the crowds as he urged them sometimes in English and at other times in eloquent Irish, but always with impassioned earnestness to "flee from the wrath to come."

In his 76th year (note this well, preacher) he says, "I preached six and thirty times in sixteen days." He later records, that "from Sunday morning, August 27, to Thursday morning, September 21, I was enabled by my Lord to preach fifty-four times in and out of doors-not far off from my seventy-seventh year!"

A year short of his eightieth birthday, Gideon Ousely died—full of wisdom, full of years, full of grace. Devout men carried him to his resting place, a grave on Mount Jerome, and "there returned to mother earth all that was now earthly of one of the best sons of Erin that the green sod ever covered."

Chapter 25

Billy Nicholson

The Irish Whitefield

IN THE YEAR 1900 a "massed band" of four people marched out-of-step down the main street of Bangor in Northern Ireland. The two members with uniforms were Salvation Army lassies; the other two were young men. One of these men had a mind keen as a razor's edge; the other (according to the first) "hadn't enough brains to give him a nucleus for a headache."

The young man who headed this little parade was beating a tuneless tambourine. He had recently vowed that for Christ's sake he would go anywhere and do anything at any cost. Then this silly thing in the streets of his hometown had turned up. He had been walking down the street when this Salvation Army lassie asked him to stand with the other three at the street corner to witness for Christ.

It hadn't the faintest smell of the heroic about it. Theories he formulated in the armchair looked heroic. But in the heat of the battle, a swivel-chair theologian's theories perish. For this young man it was tough to get things in line when he actually faced his Goliath.

"Daft Jimmy," the nitwit who stood with the sally lassies, wore a red jersey. On the back of it in white letters was written the startling non-scriptural text, "Saved from Public Opinion." Maybe the nitwit hadn't enough wit to be scared of anybody, but the young leader was scared. Moreover, wide-eyed cynics showered the band with unsubdued catcalls. What a baptism! His public enemy number one was public opinion. His meeting with God had been a mountaintop experience. Now he was in the valley of humiliation.

To make bad worse (as the Irish say it), it seemed by some pre-arranged signal that every friend, every relative, and every enemy of his passed the corner as he stood there bashfully. Notice that I said "passed"—thus marking the meeting's total ineffectiveness.

Seeing the dilemma, one of the Army lassies suggested that the four kneel down and ask the Lord to "take over." Poor Billy! As they knelt there, a brother offered a "telegram" prayer which Billy wished had been as long as the 119th Psalm. Then something happened. When Billy arose from his knees, he was through forever with any sensitiveness to public opinion. His reputation died and had a public funeral in that street meeting. (To die and be buried publicly doesn't take long!)

To the jeering spectators, this street meeting may have looked like comedy. But to this young man it was sweeter than the "Triumphal March" in Verdi's "Aida." It was a glory march to celebrate a greater victory to him than that of Nelson at Trafalgar or King William III at the

Battle of the Boyne. Billy was triumphant. He had just lost what he never wanted to find again and had just found what he never wanted to lose. He lost his reputation and fear of man and found the joy and peace of the overflowing fullness of the Spirit. Hallelujah!

That meeting was his inauspicious comic introduction into a world of evangelism. Who was this young man? None other than W.P. Nicholson (better known to millions as just W.P.). He was as Irish as the turf and rugged as the hills of Donegal.

W.P.'s middle initial might well have been "C" for courage. At fifteen he sailed away from home as an apprentice seaman. His was a harsh training. He had been at sea in old sailing vessels as long as five months at a time without seeing land. He had weathered Cape Horn in a hurricane. He had fought overweight men bare fisted. His fighting was "all in and no holds barred."

W.P. was saved in 1899 and he knew it. Months later (and only a few hours before his famed street meeting episode in Bangor) he had had an old-fashioned liberation from sin. Presbyterian though he was-full-blooded, pedigreed, and blue-stockinged-after the Spirit liberated him, he began to weep and sing and rejoice like any old-fashioned Free Methodist.

Because of his meetings, many men are in the ministry today, battering the strongholds of Satan and snatching souls from the burning. One of these was my friend, Andy Mays, the old drunk who was saved in Billy's meeting.

The first night Andy Mays attended the meeting, he itched on his chair. "Nicholson won't get me in there again," he vowed as he left the service. But the next night Andy was there. As he left, he repeated his vow. The third night Andy sat way up on the "top deck." But the higher you are, the further you fall. That night Andy fell right into the hands of a merciful God.

Andy lived effectively in "Beach House," outside a town called Lisburn, nine miles from Belfast. Andy has walked long and well. But the evangelist who showed him "yonder shining light" (as Bunyan said) was Billy Nicholson.

W.P. became a fearless and flaming winner of souls. He was enthusiastic and effective. The Bible became his textbook and his greatest delight was witnessing for his Savior and winning souls.

Wilbur Chapman and Charles Alexander asked him to accompany them to Australia. As in Ireland, so in Australia; there were mighty moves of the Spirit. Later on Peter Connolly teamed with him. Tens of thousands came to Christ as Savior, and uncounted more numbers knew for themselves the Spirit-filled life, through his preaching.

There were also great times when Finney, Billy Sunday, Dr. Torrey, and W.P. used the Sunday afternoons in meetings for men only. One minute the men were sore with laughing; minutes later they were shaking with conviction. W.P. could play on the human emotions, fears, and mind as Mendelssohn played the organ.

Very few Christians have known the craft of evangelism better than Nicholson. He prayed, he studied, he wept, he warned, he pleaded, he urged, he coaxed, he threatened. He would be "all things to all men that he might by all means save some." When he entered a pulpit, he did so with "soul-sweat." It would be no exaggeration to say "the gates of hell could not prevail against him."

One instance of his preaching can be seen the time he gave a great message on John 3:16. At the invitation to accept God's love, there was not a move. W.P.'s guns were loaded the next night with a fearful message on hell. No jokes that night! No "by your leave's"! No sprinkling theological rose water! No short cuts! I have heard Christian men say they would go 100 miles to hear W.P. deliver his soul on the solemn subject of hell.

Billy was all steamed up because men dared slight God's love. He preached and sweated; the crowd listened and sweated. W.P. cried in the name of the Lord; the crowd cried in the fear of the Lord. After the message, W.P. raised his foot and with a solemn warning "kicked" the whole crowd into hell. "You would not take God's forgiveness last night? Then take His judgment tonight!" There was no benediction, and the solemn, stunned souls sat. Billy was half way down the street before they were aware that he had gone.

For his disgusting pulpit procedure, my friend P.C. stormed at Billy and warned, "The folk will not come to hear you any more."

"If hell is half as bad as I painted it tonight, then by Sunday night they will be glad to get out of it," replied Billy.

How right he was! At the altar Sunday night there was a shoal of souls. Conviction had so tormented them for two days that they were ready to surrender.

In spiritual and Biblical matters, Nicholson bowed to none. He was very conscious of his sonship to God. Yet he was equally conscious that he was a servant of God, and so he helped all who called for it. This was the great thing about W.P.

Many copied W.P.; he copied none. He travelled far and wide and made ten circuits of the world, preaching great sermons and preaching with the great. Yet he did not assimilate their style or use their methods. His own individual method "caught fish," and so he fished that way. As a man of God, he kept that strange originality that the Lord had given him.

Prayer might be called his habitat, for he loved to pray. His campaigns had nights and half-nights of prayer. Praying in the Spirit kept him in the spirit of prayer. From the prayer closet he mounted the pulpit-endued.

With William Burns, Nicholson could cry, "The thud of Christless feet on the road to hell is breaking my heart." Of his fiery preaching it could be said, "His words were a flame and the hearts of men as dried up grass."

Years ago devout men carried W.P. Nicholson to his resting place. Heaven knew when this preacher-prophet of Northern Ireland arrived!

Chapter 26

Francis Asbury

MANY MOTHERS have been good psychologists although they never studied psychology and probably could not even spell the word.

Mrs. Booth, the wife of the founder of the Salvation Army, knelt beside the cribs of her sleeping children to whisper, "Darling, you are not here in this world for yourself. You have been sent for others. The world is waiting for you." What an idea to send little children to bed with! No wonder all of the Booth children seemed to develop remarkable talent with which to serve the world.

In 1745 we find a mother in England who seemed a little touched with vanity. She told the neighbors, "I have had a vision that my son, Francis, will be a great religious leader among the heathen." Her statement raised some eyebrows. She said further that she was going to sing hymns to the babe and pray over him daily. Did this seem like a plot to get the Lord himself to sponsor her plans?

Mrs. Asbury walked softly with God and brought up her son, Francis, in the nurture and admonition of the Lord. While still a child, he became a local wonder in the Handsworth district of Birmingham, England. When the children at the local school teased him and were often cruel to him, he took the whole thing in his stride.

An offer came from a wealthy Christian to engage Francis as a page boy in his home. Francis accepted the job and so got free tutoring in the home with the man's children.

Francis was industrious from his youth up, for somewhere he had caught the importance of giving "every flying minute something to keep in store." This habit stayed with him all his life.

In yet another milestone in the boy's life, the watchful mother had the lead. "Why not come along with me to the meetings of the Methodists?" she asked. As a result, Francis, at the age of thirteen, had his first personal encounter with God. At that time his was not the conscience weighted with guilt or a memory stained with broken living. But he was aware of a lack of the One he did not have, and he "mercy sought and mercy found." To Francis, Christ then became a living, bright reality.

Within two years of his own undramatic conversion, Francis Asbury took to preaching. At twenty-two he was appointed an itinerant preacher by none other than the distinguished John Wesley. The light within him was not a flicker, it was a powerful beam that was soon to pierce the reaches of a forgotten heathendom.

At his own request, the young preacher was drafted to America in 1771. There he was named General Assistant, though in the following year, for some reason, he was superseded in this office by Thomas Rankin.

Then came the Revolutionary War. When Rankin returned to England, Asbury "stayed by the stuff," an act which cost him much suffering. As a nonjuror, he consistently withstood entreaties to take the oath of allegiance. This caused misunderstanding with the officials and subsequent loss of prestige and privilege; nevertheless, he believed that the Americans would win and become independent.

After the war the Methodists organized their church. At the Christmas Conference of 1784, he and Coke were appointed superintendents. Wesley grieved that these two men were later named bishops.

The secret of Francis Asbury might be spelled out by three habits which he formed. It is noticeable that they are the same three habits that were meat and drink to many another pioneer missionary.

1. He loved the Bible and memorized many parts of it.
2. He made melody unto the Lord by singing memorized hymns.
3. He was a habitual lover of the prayer closet.

I recently heard a brother boasting of the almost perpetual motion of his diesel-driven car. "It's done over 125,000 miles without a wrench on it," he said. But what opposition had the car had? The roads are glass smooth; the highways have been bull-dozed into submission; the crooked ways have been bent back to arrow-like straightness. Sitting in most of our modern automobiles, we are simply being hurled down the road in a mobile armchair. Where is the miracle in that?

My friend's diesel did 125,000 miles without fault. Wesley rode the length and breadth of England, though England is not as large as the one state of Pennsylvania in the great America. Now see Francis Asbury. For over 270,000 miles this man was rooted to his horse's saddle. Yet he never murmured as he rode through uncharted swamps. How many times he was stuck in the mud and had to lead the horse out of the swamp or escaped drowning in them by the skin of his teeth, we will never know.

Through the trackless wilderness Francis pushed on. There were nightmare penetrations into the pathless forests. Often it was impossible to find drinking water. But his thirst for souls was greater than the thirst of his parched tongue.

It was good that Francis Asbury had memorized great hymns, for as he rode along, he sang them, and they fortified his soul against the barrage of temptations that were his. Here he was, thousands of miles from his home, wifeless, foodless at times, sleepless, and more often, companionless. Moneyless? Not quite, for he carried all this great load for the princely remuneration of sixty-four dollars a year!

I said that Francis was wifeless. Both in England and in America this was quite a pattern with the early Methodist preachers of those days. It seems that Asbury's slogan, like the Apostle Paul's, was "This one thing I do, forgetting..." He forgot lots of things that others reach after. Now the others are forgotten while Asbury's name lives on.

Francis Asbury was dauntless in spiritual warfare and fearless in his journeys. He was possessed of a ready wit. He was a genius at organization and gifted with uncommon shrewdness. He had both foresight and insight.

To say that he ordained some 4,000 preachers, presided over 240 annual conferences in various districts, and planned the dividing of the great country into districts with an academy on each one, is to tell but part of the story.

When Wesley, the patriarch of Methodism, died in 1791, Bishop Coke, who spent a part of each year with him, went to live in England permanently. Then the load of care for the Methodist concern in America fell upon the broad shoulders of Francis Asbury. Gallantly he carried the main burden of it. In the journal of Asbury, the recurring linguistic decimal, "I preached," is the same as that in the journal of Wesley.

Of preaching, Francis said, "Only preaching that molds the lives of the people is great." Asbury listened to the heart of God, then preached from his own heart right into the hearts of his hearers. He preached for results. To him style and oratory were of no real consequence.

Flattery would have been lost on him. Indeed had he been flattered for any sermon that he had delivered, I think he would have thought he had missed the mark. There was something of eternity about his discourses. His own "Journal" gives this comment on one address he delivered: "I delivered a close and awful discourse; it was very alarming. Seldom, if ever, have I felt more moved."

Though sometimes dry, his sense of humor was splendid.

One of Asbury's biographers, Ezra Tipple, records that once when he gave a discourse under the anointing of the Spirit, the whole audience rose to its feet. He called men to repent of their sins. He called men to holiness of life. He called his following ministers to sacrifice. But, like Paul, he beat them all in the race in daring nakedness of possessions.

The record stands that Asbury was a prince of a holiness preacher. I wish I could have heard him, eloquent under the anointing of the blessed Spirit, as he delivered his soul to other souls. (If only he had carried a tape recorder!)

Bishop Fowler has ranked Asbury at "the head of all the Methodist preachers in America." Nathan Bangs said he was "singularly imposing." Jesse Lee thought him "an excellent preacher." George Rust's tribute to the great man caps all others. Hear him: "Asbury had the good humor of a gentleman, the eloquence of an orator, the fancy of a poet, the acuteness of a schoolman, the profoundness of a philosopher, the wisdom of a chancellor, the sagacity of a prophet, the reason of an angel, the piety of a saint. He had devotion enough for the cloister, learning enough for a university, and wit enough for a college virtuoso."

Chapter 27

Richard Baxter of Kidderminster

SCRIPTURAL pedigree is fascinating: "Isaac begat Jacob; Jacob begat the twelve patriarchs..." No less intriguing is evangelical pedigree: "Walter Craddock begat Richard Baxter; Richard Baxter through his fiery preaching and writings, begat a multitude that no man could number."

Richard Baxter was born in London in 1615. I know no date for his conversion. He "felt a great pull on his soul" about the year 1634 from the anointed preaching of Walter Craddock and Joseph Symonds.

Step back a little and get a picture of the lean, lanky Richard Baxter strolling as a teenager through the woods and meditating amidst the fragrance of wild nature. He is mentally masticating the thoughts derived from three writers of his time-Bunny, Sibbes, and Perkins. From confusion he merges to conviction, from there to conversion, and then to confession of Christ.

After Baxter's marvelous regeneration, the things of earth grew strangely dim; and he lived, moved, and had his being in God. He had in his soul the blaze of a seraph and tried to cram eternity into a lifetime.

Within four years after his personal surrender to Christ, he was ordained (1641) and appointed to the church at Kidderminster, England.

Baxter was opposed to the idea that in order to minister in the things of God a man must have the ordination of the bishops and pass through the schools of learning. He declared that he feared no man's displeasure nor hoped for any man's preferment. The latter phrase he proved by refusing a bishop's miter.

Let us now glimpse Baxter as a preacher, revivalist, and soul-winner. No gladiator ever watched the eye of a Caesar or yearned for the plaudits of men for his skill as much as this tireless Puritan looked into the face of his God in prayer and listened for the sweet voice of the Spirit. No miser ever loved his gold as Baxter loved souls. No man, trapped by human love, ever wooed a maid as this man pled with impenitent sinners. His couplet was true:

> "I preached as never sure to preach again,
> ..And as a dying man to dying men."

It might be a bitter herb for us present-day ministers to chew when we say that converts often take upon themselves the likeness of their spiritual father. Sparks from the soul of Baxter seem to have fallen on the souls that he so visibly affected for his Lord. Here is his record: "Day and night they thirsted after the salvation of their neighbors."

The outcome of this contagious passion is best measured by Baxter's own words: "To the praise of my gracious Master...the church at Kidderminster became so full on the Lord's Day that we had to build galleries to contain all the people. Our week-day meetings also were always full. On the Lord's Day all disorder became quite banished out of the town. As you passed along the streets on the Sabbath morning, you might hear a hundred households singing psalms at their family worship. In a word, when I came to Kidderminster, there was only about one family in a whole street that worshipped God and called upon His name. When I left there were some streets where not a family did not do so. And though we had 600 communicants, there were not twelve in whose salvation I had not perfect confidence."

Hear his answer to the taunt that he was idle: "The worst I wish you is that you had my ease instead of your labor. I have reason to take myself for the least of all saints, and yet I fear not to tell the accuser that in comparison to mine, I take the labor of most of the town's tradesmen to be a pleasure to the body, though I would not exchange it with the greatest prince. Their labor preserveth health; mine consumeth it. They work in ease; I in continual pain. They have hours and days of recreation; I have scarce time to eat and drink. Nobody molesteth them for their labor; the more I do, the more hatred and trouble I draw upon me."

The leading theologians of our day "work out religious theories," but—and note this well—they are not known as soul-winners. My gripe against the leading theologians of our day is that they are Bible critics lounging on flowery beds of ease and offer us, from their sinecures, mental suits of tailor-made theology.

The opposite to this was the case with Baxter. His soul ached for the souls of men. Off he went, beaming the blessed message of the blood of the everlasting covenant. He was no spiritual dreamer locked away in an ivory theological tower. Nor was he operating a theological laboratory, dissecting dead dogma. Like Wesley, Baxter was a practical saint. Baxter stood firm as a rock, in season and out of season!

In all, Baxter labored some nineteen years in Kidderminster and, as one writer expresses with beauty, "Through his preaching and the power of his holy life, the whole community was changed from a habitation of cruelty and immorality to a garden of true piety." This writer then adds: "It stands as a moral distortion that Richard Baxter, the purest of 17th century theologians, the man who longed for, fought for, prayed for, and would cheerfully have sacrificed his life for the unification of the church, should have been imprisoned by a Protestant judge and a Protestant jury."

The Act of Uniformity, which came into being about 1662, meant that a revised prayer book had to be used and that all ministers not ordained by the Episcopalian Church should be unfrocked. Baxter withstood this act and so with 2,000 other ministers, found himself without a charge. He was maligned, misquoted, and misrepresented. "In perils oft" was as true of him as the blest Covenanters, who at the same time were dyeing the heaths of Scotland with their blood.

The final humiliation of this great soul, Richard Baxter, was in May, 1685, at the hands of the notorious Judge Jeffries of the "Bloody Assize." Especially in his "Paraphrase of the New Testament," Baxter was foolishly charged with libeling the church. For these false charges this saint was fined a sum of 400 pounds ($2,000)—a fortune in those days. Until this was paid, he was to lie in prison, bound over to keep the peace for seven years. It was last-minute clemency that saved this seventy-year-old Baxter from being tied to a cart's tail and whipped through the streets of London.

After God, books were Baxter's chief interest. He wrote them, bought them, read them, quoted them, and gave them away. His own pen never dried. His literary efforts are staggering. In all, he wrote some 200 books. Another 200 pamphlets are accredited to him. He gave us a metrical version of the Psalms and two volumes of poetry.

Boswell asked the famed Dr. Johnson, "Which of Baxter's books should I read?" Johnson's reply was this: "Read any of them; they are all good." Treat yourself to Baxter's The Saints' Everlasting Rest or his Call to the Unconverted. And don't miss his Reformed Pastor. Some fortunate soul might find Baxter's Autobiography. Pastor if you see it, buy it at any cost. Also read Dean Boyle's writings on Baxter (if you can find them).

"Baxter never tampered with his oracle and never sold the truth to serve the hour." As he aged, enfeebled in limb and racked with cruel pain, he preferred prisons to pensions and the smile of the King invisible to that of the king present. No word that he wrote did he ever withdraw.

In that great day for which creation and all its tribes were made, I for one will sit in fascination as the King of kings rewards this faithful servant, Richard Baxter. His secret is not hard to find. "He was animated with the Holy Spirit and breathed celestial fire to inspire heat and life into dead sinners and to melt the obdurate in their frozen tombs."

In this spiritual ice age, we, like Baxter, also need an anointing.

Let me string for you a few pearls of other men's opinions about Baxter. "If Baxter had lived in primitive times, he would have been one of the fathers of the church," observed Bishop Wilkins.

Archbishop Usher esteemed him highly.

Lord Morley called Richard Baxter "the profoundest theologian of them all."

Coleridge speaks of Baxter's "Autobiography" on this wise: "I could almost as soon doubt the gospel veracity as Baxter's veracity...Baxter feels and reasons more like an angel than a man."

"In labors more abundant" might well have been his life's motto. Had this great soul lived as long as Methuselah, he would have given "every flying minute something to keep in store!"

Chapter 28

George Whitefield

Prince of Preachers

PEEP with me through the window of history and see the eighteenth century cluttered with genius.

That pompous dandy we see over there is Beau Nash, famed as the master of ceremonies of the fashion courts in Bath. (Later John Wesley will puncture his pride.)

The interesting character now approaching is none other than the literary celebrity. Dr. Samuel Johnson. John Wesley once declined a late meal with Johnson because it would deter him from rising early for prayer the next morning. (Note that, preacher!) Dr. Samuel Johnson's companion with the sharp pen is Boswell.

In an unpretentious place not far away is a man weaving paints into what will become a famous picture, "The Blue Boy." Well done, Gainsborough!

In another area, with sweat on brow, soul, and mind, Howard is laboring to effect prison reforms.

Over in the House, William Wilberforce, with a scorpion like tongue, is lashing the lawmakers on the evils of slavery.

Philip Sheridan, the Irish playwright and politician, is elated over his "School for Scandal." For some time Sheridan owned Drury Lane Theatre. I wonder if he had David Garrick, the prince of actors in that day, play a part in it.

Hear those heavenly strains? Here is another Englishman (naturalized). His name? Handel. With tear-filled eyes and arms upraised to heaven, this genius is singing some of the strains of his "Messiah" and interspersing it with some hallelujahs. (Is that why he was reported drunk when he wrote the blessed oratorio?)

Just before we leave the wonderland of England at this period and jump over the channel for a peep at the evil genius Voltaire, let us peep through a small window. Here is the wry face of Hogarth, painting one of his political satires which made him immortal.

Over now to France. Voltaire sits high and mighty on his throne of skepticism. Disclaiming that he is an atheist, this brilliant deist poured contempt and satire on the Christian doctrines. If he was the father of the French Revolution, he was probably goaded to it by the persecuting and bitter Jesuits lording their priestly benefits.

But Voltaire seems to have been a man of compassion. too. He was honest in evaluation. Sangster of Westminister said, "Voltaire, when challenged to produce a character as perfect as that of Christ, at once mentioned Fletcher of Madely."

So there we end up with surveying the eighteenth century with its crop of intellectuals and men of achievement. All the afore-mentioned characters have a place in the sun. Each had an art.

But what Johnson and Boswell were in literature, what Reynolds and Gainsborough were in art, what Sheridan and Garrick were in the theater, John Wesley and George Whitefield were in the church of the living God-only they were so in a superlative sense.

Here is one of those blessed paradoxes that the Lord works. Just as years back the Beechers ruled the fashion of New England, so in old England the Wesleys were a family of culture and set the pattern. Yet this Oxford don, John Wesley, is the man the Lord uses to the miners outside Bristol, England. And the squint-eyed boy born in the tavern at Gloucester is the David selected to pass the Saul and Jonathan in order to evangelize the stately rooms of England with their silk-clad patrons.

Fire begets fire. In my opinion, John Wesley caught something of his fiery zeal from George Whitefield. In this day some claim the revival, often called the Wesleyan Revival, was not Wesley's at all. At least, they say, he did not begin it. (To prove or disprove that, we can wait until the great day of judgment.)

In field preaching, the blazing Whitefield certainly preceded Wesley. Wesley picked up the revival torch that Whitefield dropped when he went to America.

Whitefield arrived in America after a battering on the stormy Atlantic in a boat that the Maritime Commission would not now license for a river trip. Again, Whitefield dropped a coal of his zeal. This time it was into the heart of Gilbert Tennant, who, we are led to believe, could out preach his tutor. (That seems impossible.) Yet greater crowds than Whitefield's trampled the snows to hear Tennant after Whitefield left New England.

Forget for a moment the other experiments Benjamin Franklin made. Right now we see him standing where Whitefield's pulpit is. Walking backward from there to where he could not hear too distinctly, he marked a spot. Later he measured the distance to arrive at the conclusion that 30,000 people had heard the anointed Whitefield at one meeting, and heard him comfortably without any amplification!

But Whitefield's audiences were not always large. On one trip across the Atlantic while he was still but twenty-five years of age—tall, graceful, and well-proportioned—he addressed a group of just thirty people. His pulpit was the swaying deck of a ship whose sails were tattered and whose gear was out of gear! His blanket was a buffalo hide, and though he had slept in the most protected part of the vessel, he had been drenched through twice in one night. It had taken the vessel three months to sight the Irish coast.

On the Atlantic or on either side of it, whether preaching to a few on a ship's hatchway or galvanizing the vast audience of the field into rapt attention, Whitefield's message was the same: "Verily, verily, I say unto thee. Except a man be born again, he cannot see the kingdom of God."

The lamp that lit the path that led to the kingdom for Whitefield was a book. At Oxford, Charles Wesley had seen Whitefield and passed on to him Henry Scougal's *The Life of God in the Soul of Man.*

In America, Whitefield pushed through the matted forests to reach the Indians. From tribe to tribe he went and from wigwam to wigwam. To get to the encampments of the Delawares, he shot the angry rapids in a frail bark canoe. He ferreted out the backwoodsmen. Men must hear the message; they must have the life of God in their souls.

From the squalor of Indian camps this seraph-like preacher moved with ease of disposition to the stately historic homes of England. Whence all those carriages? What drew those poets, peers, and princes, philosophers and wits together? Proud of their blue blood and pedigree, those aristocrats came-some of them three times a week-to hear the scorching words, "Ye must be born again."

From a lordly chamber heavy with the pungent aroma of costly perfumes, Whitefield would race off to a street meeting. Catch his joy as he says, "There I was honored with having stones, dirt, rotten eggs, and pieces of dead cats thrown at me."

Coming from Gloucester as he did, Whitefield knew that for being too outspoken on the things of Christ during Queen Mary's reign. Bishop Hooper of Gloucester was burned within sight of his own cathedral. Whitefield cared not about consequences for obedience. Tyndale was a Gloucester man, too, and think what his faith cost him!

Whitefield was of the Baxter-Brainerd-McCheyne mold; He wore the harness of discipline with ease, he drove stakes deep into his own mind. His "thou shalt not's" were for himself, and he never forced others to wear his sackcloth.

The Pope's flattering (?) words about Luther, "This German beast does not love gold," might have been said of Whitefield, too.

What was the secret of Whitefield's success? I think three things: He preached a pure gospel; he preached a powerful gospel; he preached a passionate gospel.

Cornelius Winter, who often travelled, ate, and slept in the same room with Whitefield said, "He seldom, if ever, got through a sermon without tears." On the other hand, a lady of position in New York said, "Mr. Whitefield was so cheerful that it tempted me to become a Christian."

Literary men of his times frequented his meetings. Lord Chesterfield, icy as he was, warmed under his preaching. Lord Bolingbroke, not a generous critic, said, "He is the most extraordinary man of our times. He has the most commanding eloquence I ever heard in any person."

David Hume, Scottish skeptic in philosophy, and deist though he was, is said to have raced off at five in the morning to hear Whitefield preach. Asked if he believed what the preacher preached, he replied, "No, but he does!"

Franklin of America, a cold-blooded, calculating philosopher, said of the revivalist Whitefield, "It was wonderful to see the change made by his preaching in the manners of the inhabitants of Philadelphia. From being thoughtless or indifferent about religion, it seemed as if the whole world were growing religious."

John Newton, a giant of a preacher as well as poet, said of Whitefield, "It seemed as if he never preached in vain."

John Wesley comments about him: "Have we read or heard of any person who called so many thousands, so many myriads of sinners to repentance? Above all, have we read or heard of anyone who has been God's blessed instrument to bring so many sinners from darkness to light and from the power of Satan unto God as Whitefield?"

Old Henry Venn of Huddersfield and Yelling stated, "Scarce anyone has equaled Mr. Whitefield."

George Whitefield walked with the great—with the Marquis of Lothian, the Earl of Leven, Lord Dartmouth, Lady Huntingdon. But better still, he walked and talked with God. He heard what God said, saw as God saw, and loved as God loved.

An Arabian proverb says, "He is the best orator who can turn men's ears into eyes." This amazing soul did just that.

God of Whitefield, give us today men like Whitefield who can stand as giants in the pulpit, men with burdened hearts, burning lips, and brimming eyes.

And, Lord, please do it soon!

Chapter 29

John Wesley

REMEMBER the tale of the four blind Ethiopians who overtook an elephant? The groping men started to explain what they had encountered:

"Oh!" said the first. "We are on the brink of a well. I have caught the rope hanging over the rim of it." Thus spake the man who held onto the tail of the monster.

"Nonsense," said the enlightened commentator at the other end of the beast. "We are at the peril of a great snake. He has just moved his slimy head across my legs." So much for the trunk of the beast.

"You are both wrong," declared the third witness. "We are in a low cave. I have just reached up and touched the low roof." It happened he was tickling the wrinkled abdomen of the mammoth.

"Fools!" cried the last man as he held his arms around the leg of the animal. "We are in a forest. I have my arms around a tree."

It seems to me that the critics down the ages have been almost as confused in their evaluation of John Wesley as were the blind Ethiopians with their elephant.

Dr. Maximinim Piette, the Roman Catholic professor at Brussels, Belgium, terminating his classic work on John Wesley, says Wesley has been compared to:

"Saint Benedict
　　as regards his liturgical sense of piety;

Saint Dominic
　　for his apostolic zeal;

Saint Francis of Assisi
　　for his love of Christ and for his detachment
　　from the world;

Ignatius of Loyola
　　for his genius as an organizer."

The distinguished political leader and man of letters Augustine Birrel does not hesitate to call John Wesley "the greatest force of the eighteenth century."

Canon J. Overton, the Anglican historian, might be charged with being a little biased in his view of his fellow Anglican, but he rates Wesley as "the busiest, and in some respects, the most important life in that century."

Dr. T.R. Glover, the Public Orator Emeritus of Cambridge University, England, places Wesley with Paul, Augustine, and Luther, thus ranking him with the greats of the evangelical succession.

As I see it, Wesley might have been the Prime Minister of England had he turned his genius into political channels. He might have forestalled many of the later inventors had he applied himself to the tricks of science. His bank balance at death might have been like that of a Rothschild had he devoted his gifts to the unrighteous mammon.

Peep for a moment at the antecedents to John Wesley's conversion. His diary gives these illuminating facts:

"In the year 1725, being in the 23rd year of my age, I met with Bishop Taylor's Rules and Exercises of Holy Living and Dying. I was exceedingly affected. I resolved to dedicate my life to God. A year or two after Mr. Law's Christian Perfection was put into my hands. This convinced me more than ever of the impossibility of being half Christian. And I am determined, through His grace (the absolute necessity of which I was deeply sensible) to be all devoted to God—to give Him all my soul, my body and my substance."

. Despite this startling word from his own pen, plus the fact that this good soul rose at four a.m. to pray, besides giving alms and devotedly caring for the poor—yet he owns to having no witness of the Spirit that he was born of God.

About midnight on the 24th of August, 1709, while he was not yet six years of age, John Wesley was dramatically saved from his burning home. On the 24th of May 1738, mature, educated, self-disciplined, and virtuous by any standard, Wesley was saved again. About a quarter to nine on that memorable night John Wesley's heart was strangely warmed, and because of that, the world has been warmer ever since.

As a brand plucked from the burning, Wesley went forth to pluck other brands from eternal burnings. The dignified, dapper Oxford don saddled his mare and with eager pity sought the "erring children, lost and lone."

Darkness covered England and gross darkness her people when Wesley, along with Whitefield, picked up the torch of Biblical regeneration to light her thickest gloom.

Bishops Butler and Berkley have been called the best churchmen of their day; nevertheless Butler forbade Wesley and Whitefield to preach in his diocese although it was thronged with some of the most degraded folk in the kingdom.

There were ministers with hearts aflame in other parts of England at the time, notably Grimshaw of Haworth (he was our portrait number three). William Law was Wesley's contemporary theologian at the same time that Charles Wesley, Phillip Dodderidge, and Isaac Watts were putting divine fire into music and setting spiritual truth to song.

It amazes me that the Lord took the tender and scholarly Wesley to the outcasts of men and then took Whitefield from the tavern atmosphere where he was raised to evangelize the elite in their silks and satins.

Wesley as a preacher is described in a paragraph I often read from the pen of an unknown author.

"Take thy liberty; occupy thy commission, wound and heal; break down and build up again. Be fettered by no times; accommodate no man's conveniency; spare no man's prejudice; yield to no man's inclinations though thou scatter all thy friends and rejoice all thine enemies. Preach the gospel: not the gospel of the last age or of this age, but the everlasting gospel."

I believe that this is just what Wesley did.

Wesley probably lacked both the oratory and some of the fire of Whitefield, but no one has ever seriously questioned his anointing. Wesley had power, and under his preaching men were slain of the Lord. Even the boisterous Whitefield was alarmed at this, but he was more alarmed when, within days, the same phenomena attended his own meetings.

John Wesley preached with revelation. "His spiritual insight was hardly less than terrible. He seemed to see into men's souls, to put his finger upon the hidden sin, the unconfessed fear."

In the main, the unchurched people loved to hear him. In nine months he delivered at least five hundred sermons, and only six of them in churches.

Mr. Wesley did preach second-blessing holiness. Hear him in writing to Joseph Benson: "With all zeal and diligence confirm the brethren (1) in holding fast that whereto they have attained-namely, remission of all their sins by faith in the bleeding Lord, and (2) in expecting a, 'second change,' whereby they shall be saved from all sin and perfected in love."

To Sarah Rutter he writes: "Gradual sanctification may increase from the time you are justified, but full deliverance from sin, I believe, is always instantaneous-at least, I never knew an exception."

Space forbids more about this flaming apostle. Let me conclude with Dr. W. H. Fitchett's words on this God-possessed soul:

"He seemed to live many lives in one, and each life was of an amazing fullness. He preached more sermons, traveled more miles, published more books, wrote more letters (without a secretary), built more churches, waged more controversies, and influenced more lives than any other man in English history. And through it all, as he himself in a humorous paradox puts it, he had not time to be in a hurry."

John Wesley was "a good man, full of faith and of the Holy Ghost."

Chapter 30

Savonarola

The Fearless Florentine

IN APRIL, 1492, in Florence, Italy, amid the mocking vanity of his palatial villa, lay the dying Lorenzo de Medici, better known to historians as Lorenzo the Magnificent. His face was sculptured with torture, his mind was heavy with fears, his soul was borne down with a regiment of sins. For decades Lorenzo had fared sumptuously. He had fought with many, and almost always come away the victor. He purposed to live on in sin and with more laurels for his lofty head. One thing alone balked the wealthy potentate from the goal. The rider of the pale horse, Death, had come to claim his own. Though patron of the arts, poet, scholar, statesman, and designer of some of the wildest, gayest bacchavilian carnivals of all time, he must die.

On his deathbed there was one straw of comfort for Lorenzo. The pope, none other than the foul, completely corrupt Alexander VI, shared the humiliation of finding one man untarnished by threat and unmoved by intimidation.

Alexander VI was the notorious Roderigo Borgia, of whom it was said, "No offender who was ever invited by

Roderigo Borgia to the Vatican ever returned from Rome. Behind the Saint Angelo Castle were horrible dungeons, walled-up cells, and famed Spanish iron collars. Poison and knife were always close at hand in Pope Alexander's court."

One person alone had withstood the mighty Medici Lorenzo, and he was a monk—the fearless Girolamo Savonarola of Florence, a man of God who had no price tag.

To his eye the priceless immortal frescoes on the cathedral walls offered no solace. Tell him, if you will, that they were spun from shapeless paint by the crafty fingers of the famed Fra Angelico, and the news will lift neither his eyes nor his spirit. Even the gold-crusted psaltery in his hand has folded before the tear-dimmed eyes of this prophet.

Picture this reformer: unattractive, maybe, he was a small man with fiery inspiring eyes, olive skin, hooked nose, somber appearance, and dreadful earnestness. He is leaning hard over the pulpit of the cathedral. His brow is mitered with a holy nimbus, his eyes ablaze with a fearsome penetration, his weighty mind fertile with God-inspired thought.

I remind you of the words of the saintly Robert Murray McCheyne of St. Peter's Church, Dundee, Scotland, when he said, "A holy man is a terrible weapon in the hands of a holy God."

The sting of a scorpion's tail is a comfortable thing in comparison with the fire-tipped tongue of Savonarola the prophet-reformer.

Savonarola's trumpet-voice echoed all the way to the Vatican and from there through the corridors of hell itself. At the other-world authority of the man, pope, priests, princes, people, and the prince of darkness himself trembled.

Savonarola vexed his righteous soul every day as an unwilling spectator of the shameless violations of the laws of man and God. He dominated the living of the Florentines. Under the crafty, carnal rulership of the Medici tyrants, Florence had reached the apex in licentiousness and corruption.

At that time, "Venus had become a goddess of art; Plato a god of letters; Cicero an apostle; and Virgil a canonized saint. Cardinal Bembo warned the people against reading St. Paul's epistles, for their 'barbarous style' would corrupt the refined, classical taste. He commended instead the reading of Cicero. Dante's Divina Comedia was announced to be inferior to Lorenzo's immortal and fake Canti Carnascialaschi. Aristotle was more important than the Bible." All this, mark you, was called the age of refined taste.

The political reforms of the fearless priest were merely getting his foot in the door. Next came the effort to "cleanse the temple." This, I think, was like trying to scrub a mud floor.

There may soon be martyr fire before Savonarola, but another fire—Holy Ghost fire—burns within the heart of this man elected of God to make the Calvary charge against the machinations of the devil.

The church's trappings and turrets he sees not. The red hat of a cardinal offered by the smarting Pope, he contemptuously disdains with the caustic comment. "No hat will I have but that of a martyr, reddened with my own blood." (He got exactly that in his final hours.)

To this enlightened man there has come a new awareness that God is of holier eyes than to behold iniquity. Thus enlightened, he roars, "The earth teems with bloodshed. Yet the priests take no heed; rather by their evil example they bring spiritual death upon all. They have withdrawn from God. Their piety consists in spending their nights with harlots and all their days in chattering in choirs, and the altar is made a place of traffic for the clergy. They say that God hath no care of the world, that all cometh by chance. Neither believe they that Christ is present in the sacrament.

"'Come here, thou ribald church,' the Lord said; 'I gave thee beautiful vestments, but thou hast made idols of them. Thou hast dedicated the sacred vessels to vain glory, the sacraments to simony; thou hast become a shameless harlot in thy lusts; thou art lower than a beast; thou are a monster of abomination. Once, thou felt shame for thy sins, but now thou art shameless. Once, anointed priests called their sons nephews; now they speak no more of their nephews, but always and everywhere of their sons. Everywhere thou hast made a public place and raised a house of ill fame. And what doeth the harlot? She sitteth on the throne of Solomon and soliciteth all the world; he that hath gold is made welcome and may do as he will; but he that seeketh to do good is driven forth!"

"Oh Lord my Lord, they will allow no good to be done! And thus, O prostitute church, thou hast displayed thy foulness to the whole world, and stinketh unto heaven. Thou hast multiplied thy fornications in Italy, in France, in Spain, and all other parts.

" 'Behold, I will put forth My hand,' saith the Lord, 'I will smite thee, thou infamous wretch; My sword shall fall on thy children, on thy house of shame, on thy harlots, on thy palaces, and My justice shall be made known. Earth and heaven, the angels, the good and the wicked all shall accuse thee, and no man shall be with thee; I will give thee unto thine enemies' hands.'

"O priests and friars, ye, whose evil example hath entombed this people in the sepulcher of ceremony, I tell ye this sepulcher shall be burst asunder, for Christ will revive His church in His Spirit."

Carnality cringed and conspired at this tirade. Angry enemies, concerned friends, and envious Franciscan monks viewed the efforts of the righteous Savonarola with suspicion, ridicule, or fear.

"What right had a priest to dictate civil laws?" they cried. Can this man render to God the things that are Caesar's?

The potentates of the church tried everything lawful or otherwise to divert this blazing soul from his goal. For awhile all failed. Finally Pope Alexander excommunicated Savonarola.

After the decree that the saint be defrocked, the adulating crowd, which had been transfixed for years by his preaching, poured their abuse on him. As he left Saint Mark's, where he preached his last sermon, the folks hurled rocks at him. They booed and hissed. One angry soul wrenched the reformer's arm from its socket.

For Savonarola this was but the beginning of sorrows.

Later, by orders from the "holy" man at Rome, Savonarola was stretched on the rack. Another sport they played with him was to string him up high with a rope, then letting the thing go, they watched this clean man of God hurl to the ground. This "gracious" treatment was done not less than thirteen times one day.

Gallows were erected; beneath the gallows, fires were started. Pope Alexander sent a special message of "comfort" to the condemned reformer. A papal commissioner cried to the dying hero, "I exclude thee from the militant and triumphant church."

The unflinching soul on the smoke-wretched gallows answered, "From the church militant thou mayest, but from the church triumphant thou canst not." In that blessed hope Savonarola died.

God send us men of his faith, fire, and fearlessness in our awful hour.

9 780983 810575